VOLUME 1

CIVIC LITERACY

VOLUME 1

CIVIC LITERACY

BUILDING CIVIC FUTURES IN K–12 CLASSROOMS

EDITORS
Stephanie M. Robillard, Saint Mary's College of California
Nicole Mirra, Rutgers University
Antero Garcia, Stanford University

NCTE National Council of Teachers of English®

Copy editor: Michael Ryan
Staff editor: Cynthia Gomez
Cover design: Pat Mayer
Interior design: Ash Goodwin

ISBN 978-0-8141-0231-2
eISBN 978-0-8141-0233-6
PDF ISBN 978-0-8141-0235-0

It is the policy of NCTE in its journals and other publications to provide a forum for the open discussion of ideas concerning the content and the teaching of English and the language arts. Publicity accorded to any particular point of view does not imply endorsement by the Executive Committee, the Board of Directors, or the membership at large, except in announcements of policy, where such endorsement is clearly specified.

NCTE provides equal employment opportunity to all staff members and applicants for employment without regard to race, color, religion, sex, national origin, age, physical, mental or perceived handicap/disability, sexual orientation including gender identity or expression, ancestry, genetic information, marital status, military status, unfavorable discharge from military service, pregnancy, citizenship status, personal appearance, matriculation or political affiliation, or any other protected status under applicable federal, state, and local laws.

Every effort has been made to provide current URLs and email addresses, but, because of the rapidly changing nature of the web, some sites and addresses may no longer be accessible.

Library of Congress Control Number: 2024948864

DEDICATION

This volume is dedicated to the memory of Tamir Rice, 2002–2014.

VOLUME 1 | BUILDING CIVIC FUTURES IN K–12 CLASSROOMS

CONTENTS

INTRODUCTION

More than "Adults-in-the-Making": Civic Education as a Counter to Adult Supremacy

On July 21, 2024, Google searches for Alexandria Ocasio-Cortez's age peaked. This was the same day President Joe Biden tweeted that he was declining the presidential nomination. Was Ocasio-Cortez eligible to run for president of the United States? At the time, the United States Representative was thirty-four, and, indeed, too young to run for the nation's highest office. While she would turn thirty-five prior to taking office, in order to declare her candidacy, she would have to already be thirty-five years old, whereas Biden, almost fifty years her senior, was still eligible to run for office. The peak in Google searches highlighted a unique orientation toward age in the United States: the common existence of minimum age requirements for participation in civic activities (jury duty, voting, military service) but relatively few mandatory retirement ages. In fact, the Age Discrimination Employment Act (ADEA) of 1967 specifically focuses on work discrimination *against people over forty*. Codified into the law is a concept youth activists call "adult supremacy"—a system in which adults' ambitions, privileges, and needs are prioritized over those of minors (Distro, 2019). Also referred to as adultism, youngism, and youth oppression, adult supremacy is also defined as a "power position in which adult interests consciously or unconsciously trump child wellbeing" (Aware, 2020). To be clear, AOC is an adult, and her ineligibility to run for president is not an example of adult supremacy. However, her inability to serve simply because of her age is an example of how ageism works against younger people as well, particularly when it comes to civic engagement.

This volume of civic learning opportunities with and for young people centers the possibilities of engaging learners meaningfully and recognizing their existing forms of expertise and interests. Consisting of twelve chapters from researchers and educators across the United States and Canada, this volume outlines how educators have shifted the lens away from a civics education that informs an adult-dictated orientation to the work and instead engages youth in imagining and creating the world they want to inhabit. It is an approach that resists adult supremacy and recognizes that children and youth have ideas and thoughts about how to engage meaningfully in their world.

More than three decades ago, educator and author Alfi Kohn (1993) wrote, "Children, after all, are not just adults-in-the-making. They are people whose current needs and rights and experiences must be taken seriously" (p. 12). His words were an invitation and challenge to educators to see children in their full humanity—as capable beings with needs and wants and abilities that should be respected. We, too, hold seriously the dreams, hopes, and ideas of youth and believe that classrooms should be a place where they are afforded the opportunity to imagine and enact better worlds that are aligned with these dreams.

Adult Supremacy, Childhood, and the Eye of the Beholder

Adult supremacy manifests in a myriad of ways. For example, children are often lifted off the ground (picked up) without their consent because of their size, regardless of what the child wants, or they are required to bestow physical affection on someone, even being chided for refusing parental requests. These physical manifestations of adult supremacy remove or restrict the agency of the child. Expressions used with teenagers such as "I'm doing this for your own good" and "you'll understand when you are older" are also representations of adult supremacy; they disregard the intellectual capacities of youth to understand and make sense of the logics of the adults around them. Adolescents, as they begin to assert their own ideas and hold greater regard for their friends' values and beliefs, may feel the sting of adult supremacy more so than their younger counterparts. And they may be correct in their desire to be treated with greater liberty than their parents and guardians would choose to allow—particularly since ideas around adolescence are socially constructed and influenced by white supremacy and ableism.

Our understanding of human development, and in this case child and adolescent development, is influenced by the communities in which people live. Barbara Rogoff's (2003) influential text *The Cultural Nature of Human Development* features two pictures of children performing skilled tasks—in one, a six-year-old girl is holding her infant cousin, and in the other, an eleven-month-old boy is standing and using a machete to cut fruit. Both pictures might cause alarm for readers in the United States, but they lead to fundamental questions: At what age is a child able to take care of another child and when can a child be trusted with a knife? Rogoff (2003) reminds readers that some cultural communities "may regard 'timetables' of development in other communities as surprising or even dangerous" (p. 4). Such timetables clearly function and fluctuate in the United States, where a fourteen-year-old living in South Dakota can qualify for a driver's license. Yet if that same teen moves to New Jersey, they would need to wait another three years until they could legally drive there (*Driving Age by State*, 2024). In Vermont, there is no age limit to own a shotgun or rifle, but one needs to be sixteen to legally own a handgun (without parental consent). In California, they must be eighteen ("Minimum Age," 2024).

Whether a youth is perceived as a youth is also a matter of cultural influence and, for some, tied to white supremacy. Goff et al.'s (2014) study on perceptions of African American youth demonstrated that they are often perceived to be 4.5 years older than their actual age—making a ten-year-old boy perceived to be almost fifteen. In contrast, white children are afforded the freedom to be in the fullness of their childhood identities without being perceived as older. Additionally, Black youth are also often perceived by white people as dangerous (Todd et al., 2016). To view a preteen boy playing with a water gun in a park as a "real and active threat" (Gorman, 2015) speaks to Black boys (and Black men) being perceived as dangerous and violent and is an example of white supremacy.

In 2018, Georgetown University published a report documenting the myriad ways that Black girls are routinely denied the experiences afforded to white girls. They were viewed as needing less protection and less nurturing, and they were seen as more independent and more knowledgeable about adult topics. This difference in perception manifests in schools as Black girls are disciplined for dress code violations at a higher rate than their white counterparts (Epstein et al., 2017). These perceptions about Black children are rooted in enslavement, a time in which Black children were expected to labor as soon as they could walk and whose personhoods were consistently commodified. Such ideas about Black youth, influenced by white supremacy, reveal one way in which ideas of childhood and adolescence are inconsistently applied. In this case, Black youth are not afforded the opportunity to be seen as children but instead are categorized as adults, dangerous, and hypersexualized. Returning to the Kohn quote, treating Black girls as if they are just younger adult women is different than treating them at their age with respect and valuing their intellect and contributions to society.

For those in disability communities, the inverse is true. Youth (as well as adults) with disabilities are often patronized and infantilized. This form of oppression—ableism—is defined as the discrimination of and social prejudice against people with disabilities based on the belief that typical abilities are superior (Eisenmenger, 2019). Ableism implies that those with disabilities are not capable of making sound decisions, should not live alone, and are in general in need of having (temporarily) able-bodied persons assisting them. So-called "ugly laws" were ordinances that sought to restrict even the appearance in public of people with disabilities, regardless of their age (Schweik, 2009). While these laws have all been repealed, the federal government permits states to disenfranchise voters who have diminished mental capacities, which range from bipolar disorder to traumatic brain injuries to autism (Schiffler, 2022). All of these forms of ableism affect people of all ages with disabilities, but youth are further marginalized by the very nature of their age and their status of living with a disability, and this underscores the inconsistent ways social constructs reinforce who is seen as capable and worthy of civic engagement.

Again, the purpose here is not to advocate that children and youth be treated as if they are adults. Rather, the point is to draw awareness to the way we think about childhood and adolescence and how the societal constructs we place on them can disrupt their ability and desire to participate in society. It is important for us as educators to think about how our beliefs impact our behavior and what we signal to youth through our behavior. For example, the trend of helicopter parenting, a parenting style in which parents "hover" and "swoop in" to rescue their child from any possible harm, consists of parental behaviors that signal particular beliefs (LeMoyne & Buchanan, 2011). In early childhood, this might manifest itself through selecting the child's friends or negotiating to get the child a specific teacher. In later years, helicopter parenting might appear through micromanaging a schedule or completing school assignments. These behaviors reveal beliefs about children/adolescents that may not be congruent with what the parent actually intends. The adult behaviors are intended for good, and the parents' beliefs are infused with knowing better than the child or young adult. Conversely, the youth subject to such behavior can believe that those interceding don't trust the young person to problem-solve on their own or to ask for help if/when it is needed. Extending this to the classroom, when we teach about civic engagement in ways that cover the Constitution and engage in mock elections, our behavior signals that—for people who are at the life stage of our students—civic engagement is passive. It is *pretend*. Not only do actions belie such beliefs, but they may transfer such ideas to youth, instilling a belief that their continued involvement in civic life will be passive in a government that is distant, complicated, and unable to address their needs.

But there is hope.

National programs like the YMCA's Civic Engagement program are creating spaces for youth to learn and become involved. In Seattle, the Youth and Government program supports students in active participation in government as well as sitting on local boards. Beyond these national programs that support youth, teens themselves are doing the organizing and activist work to create change at local, national, and global levels.

Of course, it is not enough to rely on out-of-school interventions for supporting youth civic ingenuity. What better epicenter for civic exploration and a belief in the power of young people's thinking that in our ELA classrooms? Considering how our curricula offer ample opportunities for students to express their civic desires and sociopolitical beliefs, we must center ours as the pedagogical spaces that are the levees protecting US democracy. We *know* that young people are full of profound ideas and civic actions, and we write this in recognition that English teachers can lead the charge in supporting youth civic voice. We need only look to the existing examples of youth leadership to see the guideposts for how to support them in localized contexts:

- March for Our Lives was an immediate response from students at Marjory Stoneman Douglas High School in Parkland, Florida. The youth-led activist organization works to "create safe and healthy communities and livelihoods where gun violence is obsolete" (*March for Our Lives*, 2023). The group organized the largest youth-led marches in United States history in 2018 and in 2022, and continues to fight for a better world.
- Greta Thunberg has become one of the most recognized leaders advocating for the environment.
- Nobel Prize Laureate Malala Yousafzai, advocate for the education of girls in Pakistan, became the youngest person to be awarded such an honor.
- Iqbal Masih, a child laborer turned activist, worked to end child labor in his home country of Pakistan as well as internationally.

These are examples of youth passionate about an issue that impacted their lives and who are seeking a better future for themselves, their peers, and those who come after them. For their labor, they encountered oppression rooted in adult supremacy and opposition that sought to silence them. In the case of Malala Yousafzai, she survived an attempt on her life. Iqbal Masih, killed at the age of twelve, was not so fortunate.

Recognizing that youth have a greater desire to speak about their own futures and the world they inhabit beyond what they currently experience in schools, this volume provides insights into how teachers have created spaces for such explorations.

In environments in which students are viewed through lenses of white supremacy and ableism, where they are relegated to being "teenagers" with the accompanying dismissive stereotypes, creating spaces and opportunities for them to reimagine their own worlds is revolutionary—and not simply via student-centered lessons. The chapters in this volume demonstrate how scripts have been flipped to allow children and teens, and yes, those in between, to reflect on their world, work toward repair, and create new ways of thinking about their futures.

The Path toward Youth Equality: An Overview of the Essays

Divided into three sections, this volume explores civic literacies from a range of classroom spaces, ages, and regions in North America.

The first section, Voices of Civic Engagement in Practice, provides readers with an aerial view of four distinct classroom settings in which teachers invited their students into a variety of project-based learning units. In "'Somewhere in Advance of Nowhere' Together: Inter-/Intragenerational Freedom Dreaming in the Classroom," Anisa Yudawanti describes a collaborative intragenerational project in which high school students authored books that were illustrated by elementary students. In "Upstander Tributes: Building Civic Futures through Collaborative Civic Making,'" Emma Gargroetzi and Janelle Bence describe the Upstander Tribute Project, in which student researched and designed tributes to honor those who have taken a stand against injustice. "'Bigger than Us . . . Bigger than a School Project': Civic Learning and Youth Media Production" by Anthony Voulgarides traces the processes of students creating mini-documentaries about environmental justice in their community. Lastly, Matthew R. Deroo, Jennifer Kahn, and Daryl Axelrod provide insights into speculative literacies in a middle school civics classroom in "Challenges and Opportunities for Middle School Youth to Imagine and Speculate More Just Civic Futures."

Section Two of this volume, Supporting Black Students' Civic Engagement from Kinder through College, focuses on how a variety of scholars center the experiences of Black youth. These chapters draw attention to the ways that anti-Blackness can pervade educational spaces and how these educators' approaches provided opportunities for new understanding and envisioning. While Black students are not present in every classroom, anti-Blackness is rooted in the educational system, and Black people have consistently fought to have equal access to it. Tyana Velazquez-Smith's "Researching Black Girl Literacy Practices in Predominantly White Schools: An Archaeology of the Self" provides insights into the ways second-grade girls, as well as Black women scholars, resist anti-Blackness in schools and create spaces for wholeness and well-being. Lakisha Odlum's "'I'm a teacher and I cannot talk about those things': Reimagining Civics Education through the Perspectives of Adolescent Black Girls" brings Black girls' voices to the forefront with suggestions on how English teachers can create classrooms that honor the lived experiences of Black girls. Glenda D. Chisholm explores Black youth activism through "demand writing"—a type of writing rooted in Black activism, in which authors protest injustice and call for changes to society—in "Promoting Criticality through Research and Texts on Black Youth Activism." Rounding out this section is Hyo Kyung Woo's contribution, "Practicing Black Linguistic Justice at an HBCU in the Age of the Stop W.O.K.E. Act." In this chapter, Woo examines the impactful power of teaching about linguistic justice at Edward Waters University in Florida.

Lastly, in Section Three, The Ins and Outs of Teaching for Civic Engagement, readers will narrow in on the moves teachers make in planning for civic engagement; from lesson planning to navigating classroom discussions to addressing student reluctance, these chapters peel back the curtain on teacher decision making. In "Asian American Civic Inquiry in Action in the Secondary ELA Classrooms," Minkyung Choi, Diana Liu, and Jean Kim provide guidance toward lesson plans that focus on centering the experiences of Asian American youth in an effort to engage students in critical civic empathy. Karla Zaccor's contribution in "Civic Engagement in the Here and Now: Conversational Moves for Democratic Participation," engages in detailed discourse analysis to examine how a teacher uses dialogue to encourage civic involvement. In "Shifting the Paradigm of School-Based Writing: Teachers Using Journalistic Learning to Seed Civic Possibilities," Celeste Kirsh describes how teacher candidates can reimagine school-based writing for more liberatory civic futures. "Grappling with the Glossary: Inspiring Civic Literacy Inquiry through Vocabulary Definitions" by Gretchen Hohmeyer examines how the glossaries in historical texts can serve as starting places for examining how and whose stories are told. And this book closes with "'Xavier for President'": Skepticism, Truth-Telling, and Self-Love as Civic Expression" by Sarah Rapp. In this chapter, Rapp describes the way a teacher responded to a single student's reluctance to engage in the lesson and how that shaped the entire class.

As you read these different approaches to engaging youth in civic literacies, we invite you to join us in considering how we can move away from adult supremacy and toward pedagogies that honor the desires, abilities, and freedom dreams of young people who are seeking better futures. Through these varied pathways, we can carve out ways to shift our practice away from adult supremacy and toward a more just world.

We close with an excerpt from poet kitty sipple's (2022) "youth ellipsis: an ode to echolalia" in which they invite readers to trust children:

> trust kids.
> trust kids too.
> trust kids to be.
> to be kids.
> trust kids to be kids who know themselves in a language that you have
> never spoken / to create languages
> that you may learn to speak if you
> learn to listen / to speak the stories
> that they know in ways that they may
> never know / to create the new worlds
> in which they want to live in / to grow
> in the ways that they want to be rooted
> / to live in their truth before you even
> begin to understand them as a human
> in the multiverse.
> trust kids to be kids in a world that
> does not want them to be kids. trust
> kids to be kids.
> to be neurodivergent.
> neuroemergent.
> neurodifferent.
> neurofabulous.
> neurodimensional.
> neuroqueer.
> trust kids to be.
> trust (these) kids.
> trust (those) kids too.

Works Cited

ACE Aware. (2020, December 17). *Our society and adult supremacy, part 3.* https://aceaware.nl/en/2020/12/17/our-society-and-adult-supremacy-part-3-2/

Distro, S. (Ed.). (2019). *No! Against adult supremacy.* Dog Section Press.

Driving age by state. (2024, January 16). Thompson Law Injury Lawyers. https://1800lion-law.com/driving-age-by-state/

Eisenmenger, A. (2019, December 12). *Ableism 101.* Access Living. www.accessliving.org/newsroom/blog/ableism-101/

Epstein, R., Blake, J., & González, T. (2017). *Girlhood interrupted: The erasure of Black girls' childhood.* Center on Poverty and Inequality. https://genderjusticeandopportunity.georgetown.edu/wp-content/uploads/2020/06/girlhood-interrupted.pdf

Goff, P. A., Jackson, M. C., Di Leone, B. A. L., Culotta, C. M., & DiTomasso, N. A. (2014). The essence of innocence: Consequences of dehumanizing Black children. *Journal of Personality and Social Psychology, 106*(4), 526–545.

Gorman, M. (2015, December 2). Officer who fatally shot Tamir Rice says threat was "real and active." *Newsweek.* www.newsweek.com/officer-shot-tamir-rice-threat-real-active-400208

Kohn, A. (1993). Choices for children: Why and how to let students decide. *Phi Delta Kappan, 75*(1), 8–16.

LeMoyne, T., & Buchanan, T. (2011). Does "hovering" matter? Helicopter parenting and its effect on well-being. *Sociological Spectrum, 31*(4), 399–418.

March for our lives. (2023). https://marchforourlives.org/

Minimum age to purchase & possess in California. (2024, April 24). Giffords Law Center. https://giffords.org/lawcenter/state-laws/minimum-age-to-purchase-possess-in-california/

Rogoff, B. (2003). *The cultural nature of human development.* Oxford University Press.

Schiffler, C. (2022). Voting rights for people with diminished mental capacity. *Mitchell Hamline Law Review, 48*(2), Article 7.

Schweik, S. M. (2010). *The ugly laws: Disability in public.* New York University Press.

sipple, k. (2022). Youth ellipsis: An ode to echolalia. In C. Bergman (Ed.), *Trust kids! Stories on youth autonomy and confronting adult supremacy* (pp. 201–206). AK Press.

Todd, A. R., Thiem, K. C., & Neel, R. (2016). Does seeing faces of young black boys facilitate the identification of threatening stimuli? *Psychological Science, 27*(3), 384–393.

SECTION 1
Voices of Civic Engagement in Practice

"Somewhere in Advance of Nowhere" Together: Inter-/Intragenerational Freedom Dreaming in the Classroom

ANISA YUDAWANTI

I reflect on the possibilities of teaching and learning civic literacy and world building on day 246 of the current genocide in Gaza. It feels irresponsible to theorize the possibilities of building civic futures without acknowledging the ongoing Palestinian struggle for self-determination and liberation from their occupiers and the heightened student action in solidarity with their struggle happening in classrooms, schools, and on college campuses worldwide. Writing from the belly of the beast, here, in the United States, it is only fitting that this chapter begins this way—as young people actively engage in building the world anew before our very eyes.

It was 9:30 on a Sunday night when I was lesson planning for my ninth-grade US history students and our upcoming social change in the '20s unit. Historically, this unit involved a research project in which students would write a report on a progressive-era social issue of their choosing. I chose to remix this assignment as the Freedom Dreaming Research Project. This project aimed to mobilize freedom dreaming as a critical learning exercise and a political mechanism to analyze social issues identified by students. It would task students with researching the historical roots of their social issue and organizations within our community that are presently addressing it and inviting younger students to carry this work forward with them. While building out the bones of this unit, I sent a text to my close friend, Amy, an art teacher at an elementary school in the same district, with a "wild" idea—knowing she was likely similarly seated on the couch, on this Sunday night, lesson planning for the day to come. Through a series of sporadic texts, I pitched the Freedom Dreaming Research Project to her to see if she was interested in building it with me and including her elementary school students. The exchange went something like this:

> ***Anisa:*** So im lesson planning
> And tomorrow im introducing a research project my classes are doing
> And im spinning it and turning it into something called the freedom dreaming research project
> And i had this wilddddd idea

> What if my students wrote their freedom dreams
> And your students illustrated them in some way
> How beautiful and wild that would be
> Was just thinking about it and scheming ways for us to do things together
>
> ***Amy:*** Anisa
> I'm literally lesson planning rn as well and I'm planning a unit for k–3 where they learn about afro futurism and create c-stunners inspired by an afro futuristic artist and we're gonna talk about our hopes for a liberated future
> That would literally be perfect
>
> ***Anisa:*** !!!!! Let's facetime this week and plan

This chapter explores the praxis of freedom dreaming in the classroom through inter-/intragenerational world building. Weaving together Kelley's conceptualization of freedom dreaming (2002) and Mirra and Garcia's framework of interconnected commitments for world-building civic education (2023), this reflective case study advocates for tangible opportunities for collective imagining in the classroom that transcends traditional bounds of school, grade level, or class.

Reflecting on his time as a graduate student and organizer with working-class activists in south Los Angeles through the African Activist Association and the Communist Workers' Party, Robin D. G. Kelley writes that the intellectual space to imagine a liberated future was among the best gifts he's ever received (2002). It was in this space that he began to tangibly understand freedom dreaming as a collective endeavor. Kelley conceptualizes freedom dreaming as an act of Black radical imagination—a process of collectively envisioning a revolutionary and liberated future (Hill-Jarrett, 2023; Kelley, 2002). Freedom dreams are not whimsical, unattainable daydreams (Love, 2019). They are shared declarations and acts of prolepsis. Freedom dreaming was never meant to be divorced from the critical analysis of the societal conditions with which it is situated nor from the collective spirit that birthed its possibility.

Within the world-building civic education framework, freedom dreaming is also pedagogical: engaging in imaginative world building, not as a form of frivolous escapism but rather as a method for sparking dialogue and new ways of thinking about the world as it is and as it should be (Mirra & Garcia, 2023). Mirra and Garcia's framework for world-building civic education in the classroom consists of five skills framed as classroom commitments that enable youth to engage in speculative world building. The framework is undergirded by beliefs in 1) using education as a tool for designing new futures and 2) honoring young people as experts of their communities (p. 10). Through this framework, networking as a commitment speaks to the social requirement of social justice.

Networking, as we presently know it, tends to refer to transactional exchanges between people to build and maintain relationships with professionals in one's industry. It oozes corporate culture and, frankly, is not something I would ever naturally claim to commit to as an educator. For the purposes of this reflection, however, I am choosing to center a more technical definition of network: to link (computers) together to allow the sharing of data, interactive operation, and efficient utilization of resources (Oxford, 1982). If the task is radical imagining, networking becomes a vehicle for operationalizing it. Networking allows us to share resources (financial, intellectual, social, cultural, emotional, etc.) that propel our shared liberatory goals. The world-building civic education framework provides us with three lenses that can be mapped onto the Freedom Dreaming Research Project that my students engaged in. Networking within, networking beyond, and networking toward freedom (p. 82) require educators to reimagine the borders of their classroom and view young people not only as singular students but as nodes within a larger network, infrastructure, or community.

Networking within asks us to first begin with the students in our classroom. It goes without saying that building community and developing trust among students and teachers are integral to fostering a safe learning environment. In order to cultivate a world-building network within the classroom, students must also be given the intellectual space to engage in collective struggles around the issues that matter to them. This is most easily taken up in content areas that naturally center these conversations, such as social studies, language arts, and literature studies. However, I encourage educators of science and mathematics to similarly engage in creating this type of collaborative intellectual space for young people. There is a growing body of scholarship in each of these disciplines emphasizing pedagogical practices that allow students to connect STEM classroom content to their lived experiences (Brown, 2021, 2019; Ladson-Billings, 2014, 1995). This form of intragenerational networking can occur formally or informally in the classroom but always with the goal of building the camaraderie required to engage in radical imagining together.

Networking beyond and toward freedom is where we begin to break down the walls of the classroom as learning boundaries for students. In addition to nurturing relationships between students and even with students in other classes, students can also "network" with future and past generations. How can elders, younger children, and community members across generations also engage in learning partnerships with our students? How do these intergenerational relationships transform how young people view their responsibility as students or as members of their community? How might these relationships change how students view the classroom as a collaborative intellectual space?

Through a three-part inquiry in which youth situated their freedom dreams within both their greater political and historical landscape and the local community, the Freedom Dreaming Research Project connected ninth-grade students with elementary school students and community organizations as partners in learning. I offer the following case study, a project my former students lovingly engaged in, not as a blueprint to copy and paste in your classroom but rather as a call to reimagine the network and borders of community that your students can learn from. I also reflect on this project to uplift the importance of networking and fostering community between teachers and community members to sustain the work of radically imagining new worlds.

The Freedom Dreaming Research Project began with a freewrite. I asked students to respond to the following questions: *What is your freedom dream? What kind of future would you build if you had all the tools? What must change for your freedom dream to come true? What is preventing your freedom dream from becoming a reality?*

Students spent the first part of class brainstorming around their freedom dreams and answering these questions individually before sharing their ideas in table groups. For many, the first two questions were particularly challenging. Identifying existing barriers was much easier than trying to imagine something that has yet to materialize. Sitting with this tension, each student took this prompt in a different direction. Their freedom dreams addressed various issues, including climate change, corruption, police brutality, food insecurity, and more. Once students identified the social issue tied to their freedom dream, they began their three-part inquiry.

Part I: Honoring the Past

In our history class, we often thought about lineages and legacies. As a learning community, we recognized that the questions we are able to ask today are a result of the struggle and labor of communities before us. In paying homage to those communities, Part I was titled "Honoring the Past." With their self-selected social issue, students began their research to address the following questions: *Where was this movement 100 years ago? Who was pushing it forward? How did they address it?* These questions prompted students to build the foundation for their inquiry related to the social issue of their choosing. For a student who chose to write their freedom dream about a world free from police brutality, they investigated the origins of policing and surveillance in the United States. They researched the political era of policing from the mid-1800s to the 1920s, characterized by decentralized police forces hired by individual politicians with little to no training, oversight, or accountability. Unsurprisingly, this era of policing led to pervasive police corruption and misconduct and prefaced the professionalization of policing and subsequent legal police reform toward the beginning of the twentieth century (Potter, 2013). Students summarized their learning through writing and answering the guiding questions and creating a visual representation via slideshow or other form of graphic before moving on to Part II.

Part II: Understanding the Present

After exploring the roots of their chosen social issue, students drew historical connections to the present. The second part of the Freedom Dreaming Research Project, titled "Understanding the Present," explored the continuation of the legacy of political struggle situated within our community. The following questions guided this continuation of their research: *How is your social issue being addressed today? What is an organization that is carrying on this legacy in our own community? How can we support their work?* In identifying a community organization tied to their research topic, students were able to further locate this legacy of political struggle within the context of their state, city, or neighborhood. Some students came into this already having a familiarity with local community organizations that were working to address the various social issues they researched. Part II encouraged them to compare and contrast these organizations' language, strategies, and goals with their research in Part I to assess progress and parallels across the century. In addition to learning about the history of the organization and its current projects or campaigns, students were also tasked with looking for ways our class could support their work. To showcase their findings, each student designed a social media graphic that answered the aforementioned guiding questions. Each social media graphic included a brief history of the particular social issue, background on the organization, its current campaigns or initiatives, and information on how people can get involved with their work.

Freedom Inc., a queer/feminist organization working with Black and Southeast Asian communities to end interpersonal and state violence in our city, tied many students' social issues together. At the time, this organization had multiple campaigns around reimagining school disciplinary policies that disproportionately affected Black and Brown youth. Their "no cops in schools" campaign advocated for the school district to sever its ties with the local police department in favor of reallocating resources toward increased mental health and family support services at school (Freedom Inc., 2017). Part II of this project led to some students reaching out to Freedom Inc. and connecting with them over social media to stay engaged with their campaigns outside of school. After the completion of the Freedom Dreaming Research Project, we were able to turn the students' work into a book that we sold at a local, independently owned bookstore. Students across my US history classes voted among the organizations they researched in Part II to decide where proceeds from the book should go. Freedom Inc. received an overwhelming majority of student votes, and at the end of the school year, our class donated six hundred dollars to the organization to support their ongoing campaigns for gender and racial justice.

Part III: (Re)Imagining the Future

In the project's final component, "(Re)Imagining the Future," students were asked to consider how these social and political struggles would progress in the years to come. In studying the history of social movements, students were quick to recognize the need for sustained advocacy by future generations. As a class, we thought about the following: *Who will carry on this legacy? How do we educate and inspire future generations to continue this work?* In our discussion about continuing legacies of political struggle, students often invoked their relationships with younger siblings, other younger family members, and future children. Incorporating their research from Parts I and II, ninth graders returned to their original freedom dreams and rewrote them in the form of a letter to a younger child. These letters would later be sent to second- and third-grade students in an elementary school across town by way of their art teacher, my close friend with whom I had planned this collaboration late that Sunday night.

For some students, Part III of the Freedom Dreaming Research Project proved to be the most difficult. Translating their research on complex issues like police brutality and climate change using language that an eight-year-old could understand was especially daunting. An invocation of familial responsibility significantly changed how students viewed the assignment. To write their letters, students imagined teaching their younger family members about their freedom dream and social issue research. Through this framing, students found language that not only felt developmentally appropriate for a younger audience but also wrote with an intimate sense of care and warmth for the reader on the other side. Following the tradition of critical race theory methodology (Birk, 2023; Griffin et al., 2014), the following is a composite counter-story letter that captures the tenor of the letters written by my students.

> *Dear Ms. W's Artists,*
> *My name is Damari. I am in 9th grade, and I love making Tiktoks, playing football, and hanging out with my cousins. What do you like to do for fun? I want to say thank you for illustrating our freedom dreams.*
>
> *My freedom dream is for us to all live in a world without police brutality. Police brutality is when police hurt someone using their power, even though they are supposed to protect people. In my history class, I learned all about the history of police and how it impacts our community today. Black people are especially impacted by unfair treatment by the police, and I want this to stop. Many people have been fighting for this issue, including people in our community, but there is still a lot of work to do. In my freedom dream project, I also learned that people are stronger when they work together. I hope you will help too.*
>
> *What is your freedom dream? I can't wait to see what you come up with!*
>
> *Sincerely,*
> *Damari*

Upon receiving the letters from the ninth-grade students, second- and third-grade students read the letters individually, in pairs, or in small groups with their art teacher. Using watercolor paints, markers, colored pencils, and crayons, each student created their own interpretation of their assigned freedom dream. Students had the ability to illustrate any or all parts of the letter that spoke to them. Some interpreted their letter literally and based their illustration on individual words lifted directly from the freedom dream (police, food, Earth, equal, love). Some students created a visual representation of their own freedom dream inspired by the letter they received (*"This freedom dream letter is about people having enough money to buy food they need, I'm gonna draw a 'free' store because that's my freedom dream . . . all the food at the store is free"*). The young artists similarly took on the task with a sense of familial responsibility. They couldn't let down the "high schooler" they were creating artwork for, and therefore they produced illustrations with additional care.

Once the elementary school students finished their illustrations, I brought them back to the ninth-grade students. Over the remaining months of the school year, I pieced together the freedom dream letters, illustrations, and student work from other units and turned them into a book that represented the labor of love of all the students in my history class that year. Through a grant from the Abolitionist Teaching Network and donations from a local community organization and an independently owned bookstore, I was able to print copies of the book for each of my history students, my school's library, the city's local libraries, and my friend's art class. In the last week of the school year, I handed out copies of this cocreated text to my students. I watched them flip through the book to find their name on the author page, their student work, or their freedom dream and pull their phones out to take photos of the pages. My students eagerly compared the illustrations with their letters and attempted to piece together which parts of the letter inspired different aspects of the artwork. In one of my classes, students asked one another for "author autographs" to celebrate their role in bringing this text to fruition. The culmination of this project was a deep sense of pride—for themselves, for their work, for their peers, for the elementary school students, and for the collective.

Toward the beginning of this chapter, I posed a few questions about what it means to freedom dream in community with others and how this can transform the classroom into a site of world building. The inception of this project was first made possible by a preestablished relationship between two educators. Amy's and my friendship goes back years before either of us entered education professionally but always embodied the liberatory ethos that birthed our collaboration. As a teacher, she is committed to fostering a creative space for her students that also functions as an intellectual one—one that regularly engages in the students' lived experiences. As a result, freedom dreaming was a natural component of her pedagogical practice. As a teacher, I, too, had to find ways to build relationships with other teachers who shared similar goals of cultivating liberatory spaces for young people. The adults have to network, too. Schools, as we presently know them, rarely give teachers the space to engage in this kind of creative work. I wonder what otherwise pedagogical possibilities could come out of centering their networking. What could educators radically reimagine together, if given the institutional space and capacity to do so? How do we embody a commitment to world-building personally and pedagogically in order to teach this commitment to young people?

Collaborating with elementary school students transformed how my students approached their scholarship. By being treated as experts and as teachers in their own right, students took ownership of their work as a labor of love. Explaining their research and freedom dreams and encouraging a younger child to dream in similar ways became a communal responsibility. Though the ninth-grade students never met the second- and third-grade students they were freedom-dreaming alongside, their existence in their collective imagination moved them to think of their work as a part of a larger, collaborative effort. This ethos underscores the type of community we need to cultivate in order to transform classrooms into liberatory sites of world building.

If you have ever set foot in a classroom, you know that students' sense of connectedness—to each other, to their teachers, to the classroom, to their community, and to the content—matters. Teachers are given the impossibly enormous task of making classrooms sites of inquiry that can transform students' lives outside of the classroom. Given the colossal nature of this task, my hope for this case study is to push us all to reconsider where we draw the boundaries of our classroom and how strengthened networks between students, teachers, community members, and children across grade levels can sustain us. This work must be done in community. The Freedom Dreaming Research Project demands that we embrace inter- and intra-generational dimensions, ensuring that we are building lineages of freedom dreamers for generations to come in what poet Jayne Cortez calls envisioning "somewhere in advance of nowhere" (1996).

Putting It into Practice

To move toward embracing learning partnerships that transcend traditional school boundaries, start by mapping your community's network. This map will help you identify the many people and places your students can learn from. Here are some questions to consider:

- Who can I build with at my school? In my department? In other departments? In other roles (after-school program leaders, special education assistants, etc.)?
- Who can I build with in my community? Elders? Other youth? Nonprofit and community organizations? Libraries?

Local businesses? Local universities?

- Who else can I build with? Students' families? Friends and family in other professions? Online communities?

Works Cited

Birk, M. (2023). Critical race composite counter storytelling as appropriate methodology to "wrestle the white beast." *Journal of Critical Race Inquiry, 10*(1), 27–42.

Brown, B. A. (2019). *Science in the city: Culturally relevant STEM education.* Harvard Education Press.

Brown, B. A., Boda, P., Lemmi, C., & Monroe, X. (2019). Moving culturally relevant pedagogy from theory to practice: Exploring teachers' application of culturally relevant education in science and mathematics. *Urban Education, 54*(6), 775–803.

Cortez, J. (1996). *Somewhere in advance of nowhere.* Serpent's Tail.

Freedom, Inc. (2017). About us.www.freedom-inc.org/index.php?page=programs

Griffin, R. A., Ward, L., & Phillips, A. R. (2014). Still flies in buttermilk: Black male faculty, critical race theory, and composite counterstorytelling. *International Journal of Qualitative Studies in Education, 27*(10), 1354–1375.

Hill-Jarrett, T. G. (2023). The Black radical imagination: A space of hope and possible futures. *Frontiers in Neurology, 14.* https://doi.org/10.3389/fneur.2023.1241922

Kelley, R. D. (2002a). Beyond the "real" world, or why Black radicals need to wake up and start dreaming. *Souls, 4*(2), 51–64. https://doi.org/10.1080/10999940290105228

Kelley, R. D. (2002b). *Freedom dreams: The Black radical imagination.* Beacon Press.

Ladson-Billings, G. (1995). Toward a theory of culturally relevant pedagogy. *American Educational Research Journal, 32*(3), 465–491.

Love, B. L. (2019). *We want to do more than survive: Abolitionist teaching and the pursuit of educational freedom.* Beacon Press.

Mirra, N., & Garcia, A. (2023). *Civics for the world to come: Committing to democracy in every classroom.* W. W. Norton & Company.

Oxford English Dictionary, s.v. "network (v.), sense 4," June 2024, https://doi.org/10.1093/OED/1709493313.

Potter, G. (2013). The history of policing in the United States. EKU School of Justice Studies.

Upstander Tributes: Building Civic Futures through Collaborative Civic Making

EMMA C. GARGROETZI & JANELLE BENCE

If you entered Ms. Janelle Bence's ninth-grade ELA classroom in February 2023, you would find yourself surrounded by a sea of cardboard interrupted by groups of four to six students clustered around large tables with structures of every shape and size made from various materials. Students gather materials, examine images on open laptops, and discuss next steps with their group. Serious tones of deliberation mix with playfulness and laughter. Frustration is also heard in an occasional raised voice or tense silence. Learners confront the limited cooperativeness of physical materials and differences of opinion about what to create, how to do so, and how to participate with each other. Ms. Bence sits at her desk conferring with a group as they share their plan and a task timeline.

In the Upstander Tribute Project (UTP), students worked to represent, communicate, and commemorate the life, cause, and contribution of an upstander—a person who has stood up against injustice using both figurative symbolic and literal approaches to communication. Each Tribute had to include a physical structure, viewable from all sides, and a digitally accessible, student-created, virtual component such as a mini-documentary, a song, audio of a spoken word poem, or a photo essay. In a culminating event, students shared their Tributes with an audience of special guests.

This essay weaves together theory, pedagogical goals and reflection, and evidence from research to describe UTP as one example of practicing civic futures in an English classroom. UTP provides an illuminating example of a project-based learning activity that exemplifies the joint calls to 1) inquire into the dimensions of civic participation through examining the work and lives of others and 2) practice civic futures through responding to the local demands of a collaborative, deliberative, and multimodal classroom activity.

Framing Civics

In examining and arguing for the civic potential of the UTP, we draw on a definition of "civic reasoning and discourse" from the National Academy of Education's recent report by the same name (2022): any collective work to respond to the question "What should we do?" about any topic (Stitzlein, 2021). The framing of this question highlights a deliberative orientation to civics, with the "should" centering inquiry driven by historical, moral, and ethically informed consideration. The use of "we" locates civic deliberation as occurring in community. Finally, it marks an action orientation in the "do." Civics involves activity. More than simply voting or learning about history, civic learning must connect awareness of our histories to imagination and action toward possible futures. The UTP does just this, demanding from learners extensive deliberation for collaborative problem solving and creation.

We further ground our attention to the classroom activity itself of the UTP as civic world building by drawing on political theorist B. Honig's (2017) argument that democracy requires "public things." She writes, "Democracy is rooted in common love for, antipathy to, and contestation of public things" (p. 17). For Honig, public things are goods or objects such as roads, libraries, parks, and schools, with which individuals in communities construct relational attachments of care and concern. The use and maintenance of these objects are defined through contestation, entailing both affective and rational investments. Importantly, Honig's vision of democratic civic life is one that presumes contestation, where contestation itself serves as both evidence of and substance for the "public" that is centrally needed as foundation for a democratic civic world. Many civic learning activities remain abstract and two-dimensional. In contrast, the UTP required learners to physically and digitally construct "things"—figurative representations of an individual's lifework for justice. Rather than shying away from the messy and even conflictual nature of the student interactions in UTP, we interpret these activities (e.g., laughing and arguing over a public thing) as necessary features of practicing civic futures.

The Upstander Tribute Project: Pedagogy and Practice

In school year 2022–2023, Ms. Bence's ninth-grade teaching team collaborated across content areas to design inquires exploring genocide and human rights. Located at a public high school in suburban north Texas and serving a mixed income and mixed-race population of just over 300 learners, the school prioritizes an inquiry-centered instructional approach in which learners weave together content knowledge and critical thinking to collaboratively address authentic problems (Krajcik & Shin, 2014).

Launching this cross-content inquiry, the students visited the local Holocaust and Human Rights Museum. Along with others, learners viewed an exhibit called the Texas Upstander Wall where they were introduced to the term *upstander*—a person who stands up for other people and their rights, combats injustice, inequality, or unfairness, and sees something wrong and works to make it right. As reflected in the museum curriculum, civic learning for justice must pair learning about injustice with learning about those who have found ways to stand up, speak out, and act against injustice. This approach supports hope and agency, critically combating the sense of disempowerment that may come from learning about injustices, such as genocide, whether historical or current.

After the field trip and before launching the UTP, learners read in book clubs about different genocides and other injustices, exploring the humanity, survival, and resistance that persists even in the face of atrocities. These activities laid the groundwork for the UTP.

Teaching such sensitive topics in Texas required communication and consent from families. For example, learners picked from a wide range of book choices but needed to receive parental/guardian consent to read certain books. In having to do so, learners gained awareness of some of the restrictions on public education in Texas and became advocates for their own learning choices.

The Upstander Tribute Project Facilitation

The UTP tasked learners with working in groups to design a museum-style installation to honor an upstander. Learners were organized based on interest, selecting an upstander from the museum's Texas Upstanders Wall. Exploring local human rights history deepened learner connections to their own contexts and highlighted that all people can make change.

Over the month-long unit, learners designed and created their tributes. They used a dossier to support this process. With the dossier as a guide, learners researched the upstander's life and work and used this research to inform decisions about how to honor them through the students' designs. In their design work, learners discussed, made sketches, and considered symbols and metaphors to communicate to a public audience regarding why their upstander's work was significant. With an initial design in hand, they pitched their designs to Ms. Bence. Ms. Bence met with each group in "Exhibit Proposal Conferences," reviewing design ideas and pushing learners to deepen their connections to the purpose of the project. She asked "Why?" and "How does that honor their work?" She also reviewed timelines for task completion and mediated group challenges as needed.

Collaboration was a central component of this project. Collaboration supports complex learning that recruits insight and ideas that can only be synthesized when brought together from a diverse set of people. While fruitful, collaboration can also be challenging. For this project, learners used social contracts, as they often do at their school, to create group norms, identify individual assets, and distribute project-specific roles based on strengths, interests, and the needs of the project and the group. The central role of collaboration to building civic futures is further highlighted in the next section, "Insights from Practice."

Insights from Practice

Over three days of Tribute work, Gargroetzi collected videos of seven groups. Gargroetzi and Bence then viewed these video segments together and with other members of a collaborative teacher-research team (see Gargroetzi et al., 2023) to examine how learners practiced civic futures. Here we share three insights from practice: 1) articulating civic values as a literary pursuit; 2) collaboration as building civic futures; and 3) making "public things" as civic literary practice. Vignettes follow learners in one group as they built a Tribute to Louise Raggio (1919–2011), the first female attorney in Dallas, Texas, and the person credited with passage of the Texas Marital Property Act of 1967, giving married women in Texas the same rights as their husbands in relation to property ownership and inheritance (O'Hanlon, 2021). The group included two girls and three boys, all identifying as South Asian. Transcription uses a dash (-) to represent an interruption or self-interruption.

Articulating Civic Values as a Literary Pursuit

The task to create a Tribute in the style of a museum exhibition led learners to grapple with values, symbols, communication, and what should be commemorated, celebrated, or remembered. As they worked to make decisions about how to represent an upstander's contribution, they identified what it was about that contribution that made it worthy of attention, eliciting specificity around ethical or moral values. They also considered how they would represent this activity in concrete as well as figurative ways, building their literary capacities. Using physical making—building objects—while incorporating symbolism required learners to elicit, discuss, and choose amongst multiple possible goals, priorities, and approaches for communication.

When the researcher approached one group about their project, Erza explained, "We're doing an upstander thing about Louise Raggio ... we're making, like, a scale 'cause she spearheaded the women's right to own property act." Pointing to a hand-drawn sketch that she had created for her group (Figure 1), Erza continued explaining her group's design for a tribute that incorporated Lady Justice with her scales representing gender equity in women's access to property rights.

> So, this is- we're gonna have like, fishing line, maybe three- maybe two, attached to a hanger. And the hanger will be like covering up, and then like, this is like, you know like those scales? The lady holding two scales? We're gonna have- using air dry clay- make the lady right there. Then we're gonna have, like, fishing line attached to the corners of the hanger. And then it's gonna be a plate with a house on it, and one will have a woman in front and one house will have a man in front. And on the back it will have, like "the property is owned by" and her name, and on this one, with her husband. So we're gonna have two different houses, both of them, the wife owns this house, the husband owns this one, they both own property. 'Cause, like, she's the one who did that.

As the group worked on various aspects of the structure, Vivek focused on completing the dossier, clarifying with the group how the struc-

Figure 1. Erza's sketch of proposed design

Figure 2. Photo of finished installation

ture would symbolize the contribution made by Raggio. In response, he and Arin discuss the justification for their work.

> ***Vivek:*** *We need to show how the upstander made a difference. How can we show that?*
>
> ***Arin:*** *By the scale, like the equal, like equal when they-*
>
> ***Vivek:*** *So, that's the difference and that's also-*
>
> ***Arin:*** *When they have the same- have the same rights to owning-*
>
> ***Vivek:*** *Oh, it's like two things, so one- that makes sense*

The use of the scale as a symbol for equality becomes the center of the conversation here, but the group incorporates other aspects of Lady Justice as well, such as her blindfold, the symbolism of which suggests that all people should have fair treatment under the law and that law should be "blind" to social differences (gender, race, class, etc.). In forefronting Lady Justice and placing a small house on either side of the balance, the symbolism incorporates a critique of the injustice that Raggio worked to undo.

As the group considered how to incorporate symbolism into the work, they also considered the public audience that would view the work. Considering the color of the two houses, Vivek used the internet to search for the "color of justice."

> ***Vivek:*** *Dark blue is the color of justice*
>
> ***Erza:*** *Aaannd?*
>
> ***Vivek:*** *We can use that*
>
> ***Erza:*** *But we're making houses*
>
> ***Vivek:*** *There are dark-*
>
> ***Erza:*** *Have you seen a dark blue house?*
>
> ***Vivek:*** *Yeah*
>
> ***Erza:*** *But, like, okay- So, like- we're doing houses. And we're thinking of like red brick houses.*
>
> ***Arin:*** *I like red, because it stands out.*

The need to consider competing priorities was part of the work as learners sought a balance between abstract symbolism and aesthetic appeal to catch the eye of a public audience that might also rely on some realism to make sense of the exhibit. Disagreement over what to incorporate into the design was endemic to this process. We came to understand that the manner of negotiating these decisions as they considered the broader civic world and how they connected to it was itself a form of building civic futures.

Collaboration as Building Civic Futures

Collaborative project-based learning requires constant negotiation of the quintessential civic question, "What should we do?" For UTP, individuals worked in groups, and at times communicated across groups, to clarify and refine their project designs. The nature of the project required learners to articulate with each other and for a public audience, explicit civic messages. Bring together a group of five or six young minds to face the same challenge, and you will find at least five or six unique sets of ideas about how to respond. Careful navigation is needed to have all voices heard. Then, with so many voices, groups must negotiate which aspects of each member's thinking will be represented in the Tribute.

Groups worked with care and purpose to ensure what they created mirrored the deserved respect for their upstanders' heroic acts. Along the way, learners navigated tasks and roles and considered how everyone could participate in ways that supported the group. While specific tasks might be taken on by an individual, it remained unclear which decisions should be made collectively and which ones individuals could make on their own. Often, collaboration entailed conflict, with multiple ideas being shared and evaluated and multiple ideas critiqued and rejected before a particular design solution was decided upon. In one example, Erza, Vivek, and Erin consider and reject multiple ideas for house construction.

> ***Erza:*** *[Explaining to Emma] Yeah, and, like, on the . . . too*
> *I'm making the house right now.*
> *It might not work, but I'm guessing. 'Cause I'm gonna paint this and tape everything up*
>
> ***Vivek:*** *Don't tape it. Taping doesn't work*
>
> ***Erza:*** *Tape on the insides*
>
> ***Arin:*** *I think it would be better if you did like that instead of like. It would make it heavier and also*
>
> ***Erza:*** *It has to be from all four sides right? The whole thing you have to rotate around it and see stuff*
>
> ***Arin:*** *We have to have information on the inside*
>
> ...
>
> ***Erza:*** *Hey*
> *Could I like tr-*
> *Could we like try making like a house out of just paper?*
>
> ***Arin:*** *That's what I was thinking*
>
> ***Erza:*** *Ya, so like-*
>
> ***Vivek:*** *No, no, that's not gonna work, no*
>
> ***Arin:*** *It would work*
>
> ***Vivek:*** *Mmmhm [no]*
>
> ***Arin:*** *Why not?*

This contestation can be understood as evidence of the group's investment in the notion that they should respond *together* to the question, "What should we do?" To complicate matters, this response must be civically, aesthetically, and logistically justified. As Erza worked to figure out how to build two small houses to balance on the two sides of Lady Justice's scale, she consistently voiced the twists and turns in her decision making, sharing uncertainty with the group and checking in. In doing so, she received multiple critiques. While this might be interpreted as a challenge to the group, it can also be read as evidence of trust. Group-mates made themselves vulnerable and expressed disagreement seemingly without concern that it would undermine their collaboration. Willingness to receive feedback and revise their processes along the way reflected the group's strong commitment to design and outcome. Erza's shifting language from "I" to "we" ("Could I like tr-, Could we like try . . .") points to the complexity of having to distribute building tasks to individuals while those individual tasks remain vested with the goals and purposes of the group.

Even at a school where collaboration is the norm and learners are guided to value the diversity of ideas that collaboration offers, collaboration did not always go smoothly. We saw many misunderstandings and breaks in communication despite the social contract, despite collaboration being an assessment category, and despite a previous semester of collaborative projects. Learning how to collaborate in school is important and is, perhaps, the most civic practice possible. Collaboration is learning about, working with, and, ultimately, changing your community. Project groups serve as micromodels of what it is like to come together to work toward a common goal on a larger scale in any and every other community we are part of. Just as in our authentic lives, even in the classroom, effective collaboration is messy, surprising, and complex. It is about building, redefining, and challenging roles and relationships.

Relatedly, as learners worked toward creating a Tribute to honor their upstander, it became clear that these heroes did not work in isolation either. There were communities behind them. There were other upstanders connected to their work. Movements composed of individual upstanders built new worlds together. Upstanders collaborate intentionally and carefully toward an imagined civic future.

Civic Making and Learning in Public

The design of the task as a maker project—one in which learners create and construct a physical product (Blikstein, 2018)—in relation to a civic inquiry positioned the "make" to serve as a "public thing." The Tributes, erected as physical objects, served as a locus around which groups became micro-democracies through investing individual and collective affect and care and connecting their local civic work of collaboration with larger civic questions related to civil rights, human rights, and social justice. Struggles over the design and construction of the Tributes created a landscape for affective investment including joy, laughter, contestation, frustration, and interpersonal tension, and this provides the stuff of democracy—necessary for civic world building. To consider civic values, metaphors, and symbols in literature or in public monuments can remain abstract or individual. In contrast, the Upstander Tribute Project bridged the exceedingly local civic questions (of collaboration) and the sometimes abstract or grandiose civic questions of civil rights and social justice. The tribute itself as an object of investment and attention served as a bridge connecting the local and global civic practice, making it concrete and immediate for the students in Ms. Bence's classroom.

Asking learners to make something in a hands-on, no-tech manner, especially in groups and especially related to a civic issue, required immense creativity, communication, and risk taking. It was an invitation to be vulnerable enough to suggest and try a design that might not work. The Tribute, as a physical manifestation of the group's decisions, left no place to hide the shortcomings of a suggested design. Likewise, there was no place to hide the shortcomings of the group's interactions. Questions about the distribution of labor could be related to any variety of challenges, including someone not being clear about their role or having no idea how to make the object they were charged with building.

In one critical moment, tension came to a head as Arin expressed concern that the group was not on the same page. As she tried to pause the building work and pull the group together to discuss, Erza insisted that regrouping was unnecessary and that the plan was clear. Vivek, however, affirmed Arin's fears when he asserted that he had not been included in the process. Meanwhile, Arun critiqued Arin and Vivek for failing to contribute to any of the tasks at hand.

> ***Arin:*** *Guys, actually, um no let's do what Ms. Bence said. Let's actually come together*
>
> **Erza:** *All right guys, guys-*
> *Come together*
>
> ***Arin:*** *Cause we're all doing like diff-*
>
> ***Erza:*** *I feel] like we all know what we're doing*
>
> ***Arin:*** *Really?*
>
> ***Erza:*** *Yah*
>
> ***Arin:*** *Okay*
>
> ***Vivek:*** *I mean, I- I'm- you guys didn't include me in the conversation*
>
> ***Erza:*** *So right now I'm making the houses, they're making the scale*
>
> ***Arun:*** *No, how 'bout?*
>
> ***Arin:*** *But how is it supposed to work?*
>
> ***Arun:*** *Arin and Vivek don't have anything to do*
> *So can you?*

Arin, Erza, and Bilal then quickly agreed that Vivek's help was needed to build the scale. Vivek's voice cracked as he entreated someone to explain what was expected or rather *how* he was expected to do that thing—the "thing" being to build Lady Justice's scale out of a hanger, fishing wire, and two plates.

> ***Vivek:*** *What am I supposed to do? That's why I asked you*
> *Tell me what I'm supposed to do!*
> *What do you mean, make the scale?*
>
> ***Bilal:*** *Make a scale!*
>
> ***Vivek:*** *Make a scale. How?*
>
> ***Erza:*** *Bilal (. . .)*
> *Bilal – talk to Vivek*

As Erza recruited Bilal to reconcile with Vivek, the group shifted into a new dynamic where each person had new clarity about their role. Arin, too, stepped into a role of her own, taking on the creation of the digital media component of the Tribute, a digital children's storybook describing Raggio's life and work.

The demands of making something tangible together created affective investments that, while conflictual at times, fed the spirit of the collaboration as a democratic microcosm. Ms. Bence designed the Tribute project to be multimodal in order to create the need for, and support the reliance on, diverse skills and assets that make collaboration necessary. From the launch, Ms. Bence worked to make clear that groups should include people who are creative, who can build, who are researchers, and who are media producers. In building a social contract and beginning to navigate roles, learners had to speak up to ask, "What do you feel comfortable in making?" "Could you all tell me how I can help?" and "I don't even know what I'm supposed to be doing" as the project proceeds and tensions rise and fall. Democratic collaboration is inclusive but also pragmatic. Learners themselves must speak up to ensure collaboration is happening. In the Raggio Tribute group, all five learners stepped up to do so.

Beyond investing their own care into the making, learners considered how to create in ways that would invite investment and care from others, broadening the public beyond themselves. The Tributes were made to be shared with others. They were created to honor an individual but also to inform and engage an audience to understand why certain acts merit celebration and respect. Through multiple rounds of feedback and reflection across groups, learners developed awareness of diverse forms of civic action and of diverse approaches to moving others to act. During their visit to the Holocaust and Human Rights Museum, learners took notes and pictures of exhibits that were particularly effective in evoking sentiment or connection. Monuments, in all their public controversy, are the quintessential "public thing." Their design is intentional and symbolic, not only to pay homage and respect to heroic actions but to foster a public through generating shared care and meaning in a public thing. For learners, the Tributes functioned as public things, both elevating the civic value of standing up for justice and acting as a site for the messiness of civic life including tension, conflict, resolution, and care. Reflecting on the project in an end-of-year focus group, one learner commented that in Ms. Bence's class, projects like the Upstander Tributes were "important for figuring out who you are and what you're passionate about." Arun, from the focal group above, added that the project "helped me learn about what I care for and what I want to stand against to help me know that who am I as a person, to know what I want to do to make the world a better place."

In Your Own Classroom

As civic-minded educators, we must consider how to enrich, strengthen, and sustain healthy communities. Transparency around injustice adds authenticity and urgency to curriculum. We treat our young adults with respect when we don't sugarcoat the many issues our communities face. Fortunately, individuals and communities have always resisted injustice, inequity, and inhumanity. Even in the face of great challenges and injustice, our communities persist. Every day, people make the difficult choice not to just stand by and observe problems that dismantle communities but to act, reigniting agency and hope in others.

Ask yourself, and then ask your students:

- What communities are we a part of?
- Why are these communities important to us?
- How are our communities threatened?

Becoming aware of issues and injustices is just the beginning of civic learning. To cultivate hope, there must be real steps to mitigate darkness. With all its challenges and constraints, physical making encourages imagination and creative problem solving. It helps creators to see how one choice influences another. When students get the chance to do this in a literal and physical way, it can lead to reimagining possible worlds.

Ask yourself, and then ask your students:

- Where in the curriculum are there opportunities for making?
- How and what can we make together?

Civic work in any classroom centers around community, and because of this, our praxes should be shared. But if we don't understand the whys of it, how can we expect our students to? Or anyone else? We must reflect, share, examine, analyze, and be open to feedback. Collaborations between educators and between educators and researchers can support reflecting on how our lessons meet our goals. Although such transparency can be vulnerable, this is the only way to build a world of education that is informed, and allow us to work together toward a common goal of supporting learners to be active participants in a democratic world.

Ask yourself, and then ask your students:

- Why are we doing this project?
- Who can support me to reflect on my process and provide feedback along the way?
- Who can I share my work with? And how will I do so?

For examples of the dossier, social contract, and list of Tributes, please visit https://bit.ly/NCTECivics.

Works Cited

Blikstein, P. (2018). Maker movement in education: History and prospects. In M. J. de Vries (Ed.), *Handbook of technology education* (pp. 419–437). Springer.

Gargroetzi, E. C., Calvin, S. L., Lee, H. H., & Hertel, M. (2023). *Learning as emergent practice in the transdisciplinary civic learning collaborative.* Proceedings of the 17th International Conference of the Learning Sciences, Montréal, Canada.

Gargroetzi, E., Garcia, A., Boss, S., Bence, J., Diego, S., Turner, K., Wei, G., Weker, E., & Yu, X. (2021). *Quantitative civic reasoning: A guide for centering civic innovation in math and English language arts classrooms.* National Council of Teachers of English.

Honig, B. (2017). *Public things: Democracy in disrepair.* Fordham University Press.

Krajcik, J., & Shin, N. (2014). Project-based learning. In R. K. Sawyer (Ed.), *The Cambridge handbook of the learning sciences* (2nd ed., pp. 275–297). Cambridge University Press.

O'Hanlon, M. (2021, January 5). Until 1968, a married Texas woman couldn't own property or start a business without her husband's permission. This Dallas attorney changed that. *Texas Monthly.* www.texasmonthly.com/being-texan/until-1968-married-texas-woman-couldnt-own-property-start-business-without-husbands-permission-dallas-attorney-changed-that/

Stitzlein, S. M. (2021). Defining and implementing civic reasoning and discourse: Philosophical and moral foundations for research and practice. In C. D. Lee, G. White, & D. Dong (Eds.), *Educating for civic reasoning and discourse* (pp. 23–52). National Academy of Education.

"Bigger than Us . . . Bigger than a School Project": Civic Learning and Youth Media Production

ANTHONY VOULGARIDES

We are more than two decades into the twenty-first century, and the literacy landscape has dramatically changed. The average teenager spends over eight hours, nearly half of their waking lives, on screens, negotiating massive amounts of information and a complex sociocultural context (Rideout et al., 2022). Within this largely unregulated space, students encounter messages about society that reinforce dominant narratives about race, gender, and social class—and urban youth are particularly vulnerable (Giroux, 1996; Morrell et al., 2015; Morrell & Duncan-Andrade, 2005). Despite this, youth are taking activist stances on consequential civic issues such as the ongoing climate crisis, racial and socioeconomic disparities exacerbated by COVID-19, and wars in Gaza and Ukraine (Beach & Smith, 2023; Funk et al., 2016). As they navigate messages online, they are steeped in a participatory culture, making decisions about whom to support, who has power, and who controls the narrative.

Contrast that autonomy with today's typical classrooms that follow organizational structures that have not changed for the last one hundred years (Tyack & Tobin, 1994), and curricula that prioritize learning facts about civic institutions over doing civics (Mirra & Garcia, 2023). These classrooms rely heavily on teaching as transmission, or what Freire (1970) calls "banking" pedagogies. Given the societal challenges of our current time, the rapidly shifting media landscape, and the need for equitable frameworks for civic education in school, it is necessary to explore approaches that might transform student learning and engagement.

Youth Media Production

Morrell et al. have argued that twenty-first-century adolescents are uniquely well positioned to create media and use it to make change, start dialogue, and have their voices heard (2015). When students produce media about issues that matter to them, they engage in analytical processes using the literacies they are most familiar with. Producing media for virtual social landscapes requires a sophisticated rhetorical tool kit. Students consider audience, purpose, and message, and employ appeals to credibility (*ethos*), logic (*logos*), or emotions (*pathos*) to be effective (Garcia et al., 2015). As youth *produce* media, they also learn to analyze the media they encounter, becoming better equipped to decode the messages around them (Morrell et al., 2015; Kellner & Share, 2019). In the tradition of critical literacy, where marginalized youth need tools for resisting oppression, media production represents a timely tool for developing youth civic engagement within our current society and media space (Mirra & Garcia, 2017).

In this chapter, I examine how media production provided opportunities for civic learning during a 2021 Environmental Justice Expedition (EJE) project. After learning about environmental justice (EJ) issues in their local community during COVID-19, students produced mini-documentary films designed to educate others and to advocate for change. At a final event, students screened films, began community conversations, and called for action. Two years after the project, I met with my former students to discuss the impact of their learning. At the time of our conversation, participants were nineteen years old, two males and two females with varying gender identities. All students were in their second year of college and identified as Latinx, first-generation college students who grew up in lower-income households. By situating students as knowledge holders, this case examines how linking media production with local civic learning provided opportunities for social analysis and social action. At the end of this essay, I offer suggestions for educators interested in making media for civic action in their own classrooms.

A Story of the Project: Environmental Justice Expedition

A critical media perspective enlightens students to the potential they have, as media producers, to shape the world they live in and to help turn it into the world they imagine.

—Morrell et al. (2015)

For the last twelve weeks, Javi, Teresa, Yasmairy, and Ignacio (pseudonyms) have been producing a mini-documentary film about substandard housing conditions in their local community. After building background knowledge through traditional research, they worked with media coaches from a local nonprofit to learn the art of documentary filmmaking. Students developed a vision for their film using storyboards and shot lists, interviewed local residents and professional advocates, and documented conditions from around the neighborhood. After weeks of collecting footage, they moved into post-production—editing video, adding voiceover, and tuning their message. At a final event—a mini-documentary film expo—they screened their film for an audience of community stakeholders, educating others about their issue and advocating for change.

Environmental Justice, COVID-19, and a Call to "Reimagine Education"

Community School (CS) (pseudonym) is a pre-K through grade 12 Title 1 public school in a large urban district in the Northeast situated in a predominantly low-income, Spanish-speaking, immigrant community. Like many traditionally marginalized Black and Brown communities across the United States, CS sits squarely within an EJ zone, a neighborhood disproportionately affected by environmental hazards and other social vulnerabilities (US EPA, 2024). Within a mile of the school are three major expressways, a bus terminal, and a substation for the local utility company. The community has long been among the city's neighborhoods with the poorest air quality, and unsurprisingly, persistent rates of health issues like asthma, diabetes, and cancer are high.

When COVID-19 hit in the spring of 2020, residents already vulnerable to the adverse effects of poor air quality were disproportionately affected. Nationwide studies found that long-term exposure to air pollution increased the risk of COVID-19 death (Wu et al., 2020), and many intergenerational households at CS lost family members in the first months. As communities were suffering from ill health outcomes, schools were dealing with their own crisis. Educators and policymakers quickly realized the "grammar of schooling" that had dominated for the last 100 years—characterized by back-to-back class periods and siloed content areas (Tyack & Tobin, 1994, p. 454)—was not feasible.

That summer, in preparation for a hybrid year of instruction, educators were tasked with reimagining education. States assembled policy councils, building leaders worked to comply with ever-changing guidance, and teachers across the country innovated to meet the needs of their students. Embracing a philosophy of narrow and deep, CS turned to a familiar structure with a track record for fostering deeper learning and student engagement: the Learning Expedition. Learning Expeditions are characterized by compelling topics, interdisciplinary connections, and authentic exhibitions of student learning (Berger et al., 2016). Coursework at CS had traditionally centered around social justice issues, and here—in this space of crisis—was an opportunity to collaborate around a common topic.

Civics Is Local

Subscribing to Mirra and Garcia's philosophy that "all teachers are civics teachers" (2023, p. 4), our interdisciplinary teacher team (English-Science-Civics) designed a curriculum to address the compounded challenge of EJ and COVID-19. Students explored questions like, *How healthy is my community? Who is responsible for protecting the environment in our community?* and *How can research and argument help foster values of self-determination and democracy?* By engaging with local community issues that affected our students directly, we aimed to draw on our students' funds of knowledge, experiences, and cultural wealth (Moll et al., 1992; Yosso, 2005). Javi, a student alum, recalls,

> This project, in particular, was very, very deep to me [. . .] It was something that affected us directly, like our community and our family.

Students read articles about climate change and access to open green spaces and examined maps that showed correlations between poor air quality, poverty, and adverse health conditions. They learned how the absence of government regulation over time helped to create sacrifice zones, spaces where the health and safety of the community were traded for the economic prosperity and gains of others (Scott & Smith, 2017). Once a foundation of EJ knowledge was established, we layered in readings that showed how these inequities—and their own experiences—were no coincidence. Students made personal connections with the phenomenon, often exchanging stories about family members being hospitalized or noting how "everyone" in their family has asthma.

In the spring of 2021, after a semester of building background knowledge, we invited our students to take action. Their task was to create a mini-documentary film to *educate* the community about environmental justice issues affecting our community and to advocate for change. Javi remembers how he felt at the time:

> It was, like—made into a bigger thing, with the expedition. So yeah—getting, like, all of that freedom and allowing

> for, like, our voices to be heard and for our creativeness and our thoughts to be out there through different perspectives rather than just words on a paper was like very, very heavy for us; or, like, impactful.

To help tell these stories, we partnered with media coaches from a local nonprofit specializing in youth media production. Students were trained on elements of filmmaking and learned skills like varying shot types (Figure 1), setting up interviews, and editing digital media.

In teams of three or four, students began the project by choosing a topic they felt passionate about and submitting film proposals that outlined the focus, line of inquiry, and importance of the issue to the local community. Some chose to investigate issues like climate change, air pollution, and urban heat—topics directly related to

Figure 1. Shot types for filmmaking

Establishing Shot	Description
	*Introduces us to a place before we go in and learn more about it.*

Part II: Framing and Composition

Rule of Thirds	Description
	*When you split up the frame into 9 quadrants using the lines and/or points to place important information--makes for a dynamic image.*

Designed in collaboration with Educational Video Center (EVC)

Figure 2. Student storyboard

Shot (what is the camera doing): bRoll_close_waterdrip.MOV, bRoll_zoompan_rat.MOV
Action (what is happening in the frame): Go through footage/images of problems and talk about them.
Audio (what are we hearing): Interview

Shot (what is the camera doing): Black screen showing the statistic
Action (what is happening in the frame): Showing the statistic on screen
Audio (what are we hearing): Voice-over narartion of the statistic (connection to EJ)

Students plan storyboards with emotional appeals (above) and logical appeals (below)

the environment. Other students decided to examine the adjacent issues like health disparities, housing conditions, and educational inequity. With their audience in mind, students created storyboards and shot lists (Figure 2) to outline the argument they wished to make. One student remembers,

> As we got more into the project, I was really getting into it, and I was, like, I love that this is a documentary, and it's very cool that we're doing this . . . . It is something I'm still proud of . . . like, I wouldn't look back at a paper or slides the same way.

Learning became relevant by focusing on local civic issues that affected our students' daily lives. By building background knowledge, allowing space for personal connections, and utilizing familiar literacies, students became motivated to learn.

Opportunities for Social Analysis

Throughout the expedition, media production afforded multiple opportunities for students to engage in social analysis. For instance, as students chose topics for their films, they began conversations about social conditions. Students recollected how a class discussion about substandard housing was critical for helping them narrow the focus of their film. Teresa remembers,

> We all easily chose that topic, because we're talking about, um, how we're all affected by it [. . .] When this topic came up about, like, bad housing and stuff, and people's experiences [. . .] everybody wanted to speak. The whole class became about that [. . .] We're like, oh, like, a lot of people experience this [. . .] we should focus on that.

This sort of informal dialogue continued as students went into the field. Redefining what it meant to be "expert," we encouraged students to embrace their position—and the position of other residents experiencing oppression—as knowledge holders. As groups walked the neighborhood collecting "street-style interviews," they reported making connections and developing a new lens for social analysis. Teresa recalls,

> Doing the research, and then, like, going out and talking to people and seeing how their experiences match up with what we learned about housing conditions [. . .] It was, like, really eye opening to see how pretty much everyone else in Bridgetown [pseudonym] is dealing with housing problems just like us.

Javi adds,

> One of my favorite parts was probably just, like, getting to hear personal stories [from] residents [. . .] I felt a bit more included, and I felt a little better after interviewing people, because a lot of the footage that we have in the video itself is from our houses [. . .] Hearing other people's stories about how they relate to things similar to [us] kind of put things more into perspective and at least made me know that it wasn't just me.

As students expanded their interviews to professionals in the field, they developed a more nuanced understanding of their topics and began to understand their roles as advocates. Yesenia recalls how "tenant rights" became a natural addition to their film:

> Tenant rights [. . .] came up a lot during our interviews, especially with the lawyers, and then with, like, the residents. [Residents] talked about how they didn't really have the power to, like, improve the conditions in their household because they were scared of their landlord, or, like, the landlord had too much power over them to the point where they couldn't, like, fight, or else they get kicked out . . . . So naturally, we felt like tenants' rights, was, like, a natural addition to substandard housing.

In a Freirean sense (1970), students—equipped with cameras and microphones—utilized the critical literacy practices associated with documentary filmmaking to engage with various stakeholders and identify patterns of inequity.

Opportunities for Social Action

As students worked to create their films, they began conceptualizing their product as an opportunity for action. With their audience in mind, students edited their media, adding music and voiceover and reducing hours of footage into a five-minute short film. Ignacio remembers,

> Like, we were really meticulous with it all [. . .] We just kept watching our film over and over again making, like, half-second cuts to, like, make sure [. . .] there were no awkward pauses or anything . . .

Employing rhetorical appeals, they crafted a message that would resonate with their audience. Students paired music, voiceovers, and imagery that would engage the emotions of their audience and then juxtaposed facts and statistics to add logical appeal (Figure 3). Teresa remembers,

Figure 3. Screenshots from a mini-documentary film

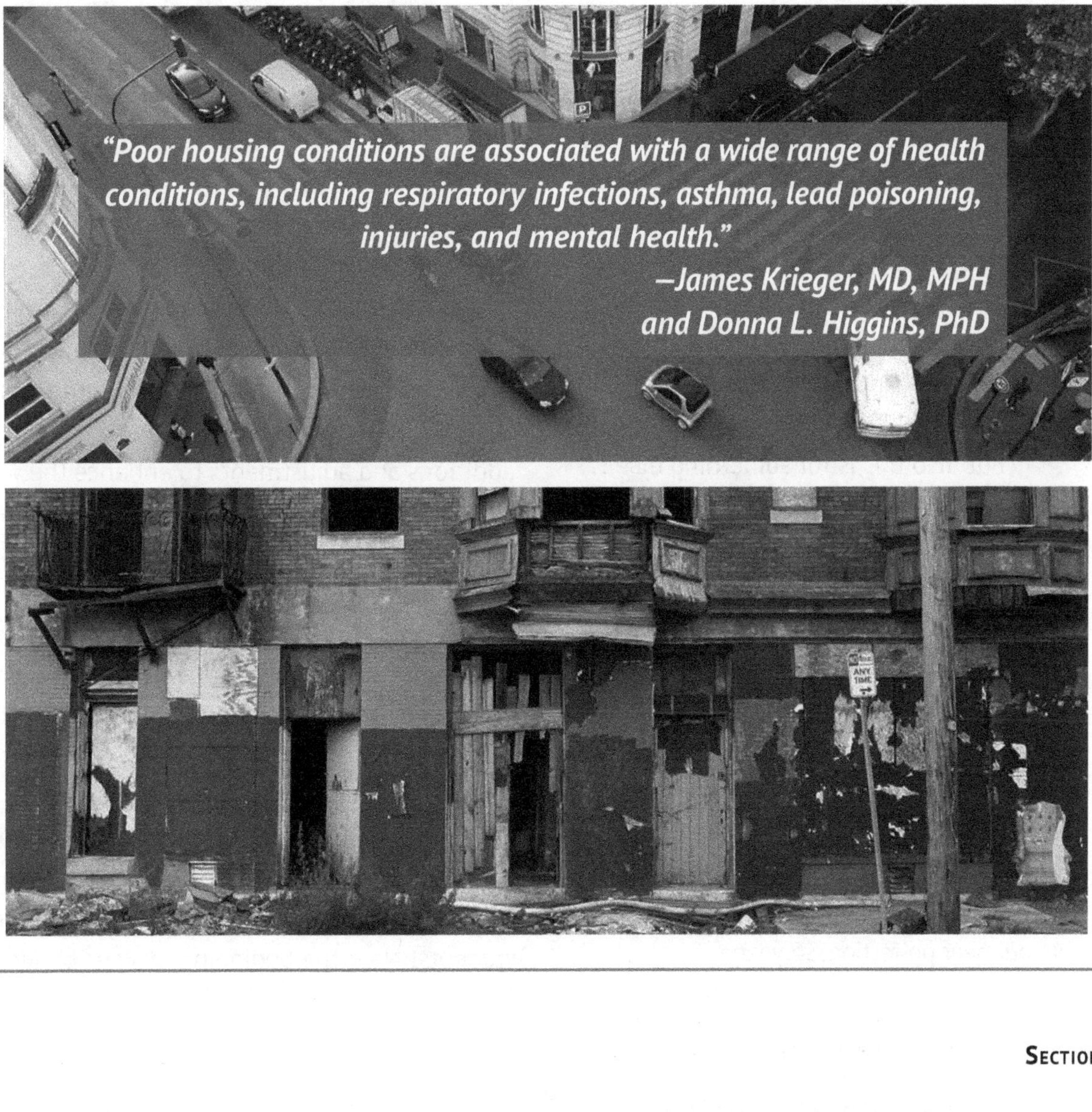

> We did a bunch of research so that we can have different types of evidence, like the statistics ...

And the group, humored, remembers the emphasis on emotional appeal. Teresa continues,

> We always laugh when we see Yesenia's sister's part because Yesenia made her .... She was like, "You have to sound emotional! Like, to make it dramatic." [participants smile and laugh] Or any of us talking in any of our voiceovers—like, trying to sound as dramatic as possible.

At a final event—An Environmental Justice Mini-Documentary Film Expo—students had an opportunity to screen their films, educating peers, families, and other community stakeholders about local environmental justice issues and advocating for change. Students viewed the public forum as an opportunity to advocate and their film as something that could have a real impact. Teresa recalls,

> So the fact that it was for something else—the expo—everybody was going to see it [...] We were being graded on it, but also this is for something else ...

Javi adds,

> For me, I ... I took it as, like, a metaphor ... just because we're starting off with bad housing doesn't mean we're gonna end up with bad housing ... and that's why the project is, like, very valuable. This is why we're making it more than just an academic thing for us[...] that's why we spend so much time making sure that, like, the tiniest little things are to our near perfection. So, yeah.

Through an iterative process of research, editing, and synthesizing their footage, students began to internalize their own roles as advocates. Teresa reflected on the impact of the project on her own thinking:

> I'm interested in policy change and being involved in my community [. . .] And projects like this made me realize that I can be a part of that, even if I'm young, because, like, it was bigger than us, like, it was bigger than a school project [. . .] It impacts our community.

Making media with students about social justice issues provided clear opportunities for social analysis and action. Organic opportunities for dialogue, interaction with various stakeholders, and the iterative filmmaking process allowed students multiple chances to internalize their learning.

Getting Started: Media Making for Civic Action

While conducting large-scale media projects with students can feel intimidating, starting small can help. Our project has been a multi-year collaboration; each year, we make additions and adjustments to enhance the work and meet the needs of students. As with any learning experience, some students will engage more than others, and limitations within one's context, such as time, curricular restraints, and administrative support, will vary. That said, below are some suggestions for getting started.

Identify Compelling Topics

What issues affect your local community? What issues are your students most passionate about? The best way to find this out is to ask your students! Near the beginning of your project or unit, spend time brainstorming possible topics for study (Figure 4). As students begin research and conversations, topics will evolve to become more nuanced. Add these to the list.

For projects that require investigation of a common topic—such as environmental justice—curate readings or classroom activities that help students build background knowledge, make personal connections, and understand diverse perspectives. When possible, allow student choice to increase autonomy and motivation.

Consider Authentic Purposes, Audiences, and Processes

Because students interact with media every day, they understand its capacity to reach larger audiences. Traditional classroom tasks are often designed for an audience of one, the teacher. When students understand that their work has an impact beyond the classroom, they become more motivated to learn and more willing to budget the time and effort needed to create high-quality products. Use formats from the professional

Figure 4. Brainstorming social issues with students

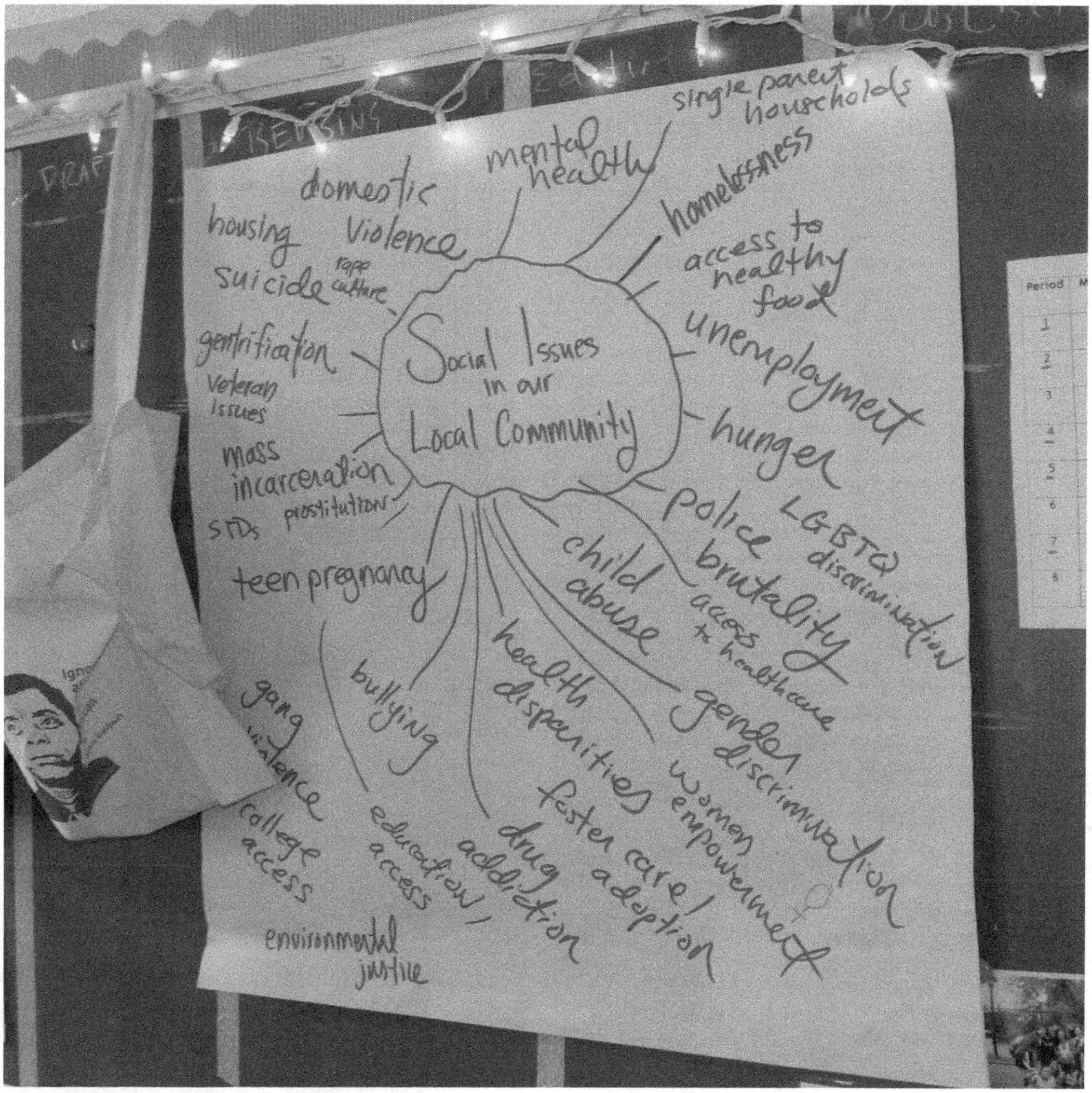

world to make processes real and to give your students a window into career possibilities.

Below are some ideas for adding authenticity to media projects:

- Plan an in-person or online exhibition of student learning (e.g., expo, film festival, art gallery, Zoom event, website, online channel, etc.).
- Publish media using online platforms (e.g., YouTube, Vimeo, TikTok, Instagram, etc.).
- Invite experts to coteach or critique student work (e.g., photographers, advocates from community-based organizations, scientists, friends/colleagues with expertise, etc.).
- Use the language of media making with your students (e.g., influencer, film crew, director, cameraperson, workshop time, rough cut, final cut, etc.).
- Allow students to utilize multiple formats and employ unique skill sets (e.g., animation, social media campaigns, documentary films, cartoons, photography, etc.).

Provide Space for Revision

As with any craft, making media requires precision and accuracy. Develop rubrics to define expectations and provide critique protocols (Figure 5) that allow students to share their

Figure 5. Critique protocols

Critique: Visuals and Composition

	4 - Exceeds	3 - Meets	2 - Approaches	1 - Attempts
Visuals / Composition	Visuals and composition are **very effective** & emulate **professional standards** A **variety** of different camera shots and movements (such as close-up, medium shot, wide angle, establishing shot, pan or tilt) Camera shots and composition convey a **particular mood** or **effect on the audience & clearly support message and story**	Visuals and composition are **effective** Includes **many** different camera shots and movements (such as close-up, medium shot, wide angle, establishing shot, pan or tilt) Camera shots and composition are **intentional and support message and story**	Visuals and composition **somewhat effective,** but may need some improvement Includes **some effective camera shots** and movements, but **may need to re-shoot or reconsider** others and or increase variety Camera shots and composition **may not clearly support the message** and story in some cases	Visuals and composition are **not effective** and need major improvement Includes **little to no variety** and **needs to re-shoot** Camera shots **do not support message**

Critique Routine

1. Prep Time (5 mins.): Prepare your artifact for sharing. Designate 1–2 presenters and 1–2 notetakers.

2. Critique Rounds (5 mins.): Each team will present a portion of their artifact. Audience takes notes and verbally shares rubric-based feedback. (praise-question-suggestion)

3. Whole Class (5–10 mins.): Discuss trends + next steps as a whole group.

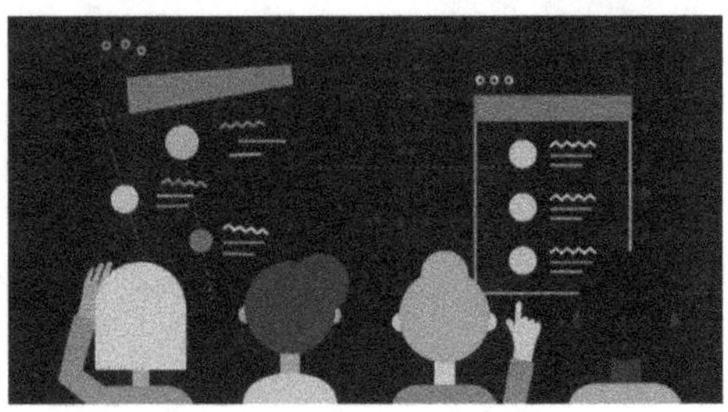

Students use in-class critique protocols to refine their work.

work and develop a lens for quality. Critiquing work in a public forum allows students to learn from other groups, understand possibilities for their own projects, provide opportunities for accountability, and promote a culture of revision.

Budget multiple opportunities for students to present throughout your project before the final presentation. It is common to underestimate how long the editing process can take, so frontload your unit of instruction with any necessary lessons and provide ample workshop time in the final third of your unit.

Use Available Resources

Making media doesn't require ordering expensive equipment or editing software. Allow students to use smartphones to capture footage, conduct interviews, and record voiceovers. Editing programs come stock on Mac (iMovie) and PC (Video Editor), and web-based options have free versions (e.g., WeVideo). If your budget allows, inexpensive add-ons like phone tripods (Figure 6) and lavalier microphones can make the process feel more authentic for students.

Figure 6. Phone tripod

Inexpensive add-ons can make the process feel authentic for students

Basic mini-lessons on filmmaking fundamentals, such as framing a shot or setting up an interview, allow students to quickly enhance their existing knowledge to produce high-quality media that imitate that of professionals.

Conclusion

This case illustrates how linking local civic learning with media production can create opportunities for analysis, advocacy, and action. To move toward a more democratic, equitable, and inclusive society, educators must be responsive to the issues, knowledge, and literacies our communities hold. If the function of education is to equip the next generation of citizens with the tools necessary to analyze, participate in, and build the society—to leave the world better than it was—then we need to ensure schools and curricula are responsive to that current society.

Works Cited

Beach, R., & Smith, B. E. (Eds.). (2023). *Youth created media on the climate crisis.* Routledge.

Berger, R., Woodfin, L., & Vilen, A. (2016). *Learning that lasts: Challenging, engaging, and empowering students with deeper instruction.* John Wiley & Sons.

Freire, P. (1970). *Pedagogy of the oppressed.* Seabury Press.

Funk, S., Kellner, D., & Share, J. (2016). Critical media literacy as transformative pedagogy. In M. Yildiz & J. Keengwe (Eds.), *Handbook of research on media literacy in the digital age* (pp. 1–30). IGI Global.

Garcia, A., Mirra, N., Morrell, E., Martinez, A., & Scorza, D. A. (2015). The council of youth research: Critical literacy and civic agency in the digital age. *Reading & Writing Quarterly, 31*(2), 151–167.

Giroux, H. A. (1996). *Fugitive cultures: Race, violence, and youth.* Routledge.

Kellner, D., & Share, J. (2019). *The critical media literacy guide: Engaging media and transforming education* (Vol. 2). Brill.

Mirra, N., & Garcia, A. (2017). Civic participation reimagined: Youth interrogation and innovation in the multimodal public sphere. *Review of Research in Education, 41*(1), 136–158. https://doi.org/10.3102/0091732X17690121

Mirra, N., & Garcia, A. (2023). *Civics for the world to come: Committing to democracy in every classroom.* W. W. Norton & Company.

Moll, L., Amanti, C., Neff, D., & Gonzalez, N. (1992). Funds of knowledge for teaching: Using a qualitative approach to connect homes and classrooms. *Theory Into Practice, 31*(2), 132–141.

Morrell, E., Duenas, R., Garcia, V., & Lopez, J. (2015). *Critical media pedagogy: Teaching for achievement in city schools.* Teachers College Press.

Morrell, E., & Duncan-Andrade, J. (2005). Popular culture and critical media pedagogy in secondary literacy classrooms. International *Journal of Learning, 12,* 1–11.

Rideout, V., Peebles, A., Mann, S., & Robb, M. B. (2022). *The Common Sense census: Media use by tweens and teens,* 2021. Common Sense.

Scott, D. N., & Smith, A. A. (2017). "Sacrifice zones" in the green energy economy: Toward an environmental justice framework. *McGill Law Journal, 62*(3), 861–898.

Tyack, D., & Tobin, W. (1994). The "grammar" of schooling: Why has it been so hard to change? *American Educational Research Journal, 31*(3), 453–479.

U.S. Environmental Protection Agency. (2024, May 29). EPA. www.epa.gov/

Wu, X., Nethery, R. C., Sabath, M. B., Braun, D., & Dominici, F. (2020). *Exposure to air pollution and COVID-19 mortality in the United States: A nationwide cross-sectional study.* medRxiv. www.medrxiv.org/content/10.1101/2020.04.05.20054502v2

Yosso, T. (2005). Whose culture has capital? A critical race theory discussion of community cultural wealth. *Race Ethnicity and Education, 8*(1), 69–91.

Challenges and Opportunities for Middle School Youth to Imagine and Speculate More Just Civic Futures

MATTHEW R. DEROO, JENNIFER KAHN
& DARYL AXELROD

In a tightly packed urban classroom, groups of middle school students sit in desks pushed together and brainstorm about pressing issues at their school. The room buzzes with conversation

> *We have a small school, with no library or room to build one . . .*
>
> *What if the hallways were bigger and less crowded, without all the bumping . . .*
>
> *There is not enough space to park cars or bicycles, we need to expand parking . . .*
>
> *Our school is on a busy street, impacting everyone's safety . . .*

Importantly, students' conversations do not stop here; they extend as students speculate ways to achieve better futures for themselves, their classmates, and community.

Introduction

Traditional civics education efforts have historically struggled to incorporate youth's ideas, concerns, and experiences (Banks, 2017; Westheimer & Kahne, 2004). Middle and high school youth have demonstrated interest in and ability to grapple with pressing social issues (Duncan, 2023; Rubin & Hayes, 2010). However, across English and social studies classes, schooling conventions, including curricular standards and textbooks, typically constrain how educators engage with youth around the issues youth care about (Garcia & Morrell; 2022; Wray-Lake, & Abrams, 2020). In response, speculative framings have emerged to encourage educators to challenge these norms through ways of teaching that speak back to deficit framings and position youth as agents of change (Mirra & Garcia, 2022; Sinclair et al., 2023). Here, we present curricular work informed by speculative civics (Mirra & Garcia, 2023) in which we introduced digital storytelling and inquiry to middle school youth in order to support civic engagement and learning.

We specifically drew from Mirra and Garcia's (2023) work on speculative civics to challenge conventional ways of teaching. We took up their questions of "Whose stories need to be heard? How can we connect with each other? What kind of future do we want to build together? How do we get there?"(p. 14) as guides for our semester-long curricular design in a seventh-grade civics class in an urban, public charter middle and high school serving immigrant and multilinguistic, multiethnic, transnational youth populations. We apply our work to the English language arts (ELA) space because of the central role that digital literacies played in our design and the relevancy of our reflections and lessons learned for an ELA context. We present our design and analysis to support discussion about the challenges and opportunities our students encountered when imagining more just civic futures.

Adopting a Speculative Lens for Supporting Youth Civic Engagement

In our instruction, we drew on Mirra and Garcia's (2023) *Civics for the World to Come: Committing to Democracy in Every Classroom.* The authors invite teachers and researchers to consider how commitments to inquiry can support students' curiosity about the world and consider ways they might come together as advocates for social change (Mirra & Garcia, 2023). Our approach was underscored by Mirra and Garcia's (2023) charge that adults working with youth consider who gets to raise questions about society or dream for better futures and what that future dreaming looks like.

Accordingly, when we first met with students, we framed our work as a way for youth to learn more about their local communities while also exploring how storytelling and inquiry are forms of civic engagement. We discussed with students how civic issues may be taken up on local and global scales and from the past and the present to the future (Kahn et al., 2022). For example, we discussed the impacts of climate change across scales, a global issue also deeply relevant to each person living in our oceanside community. We traced students' understanding of the past as contributing to climate change, asked them to describe how they currently understood climate change impacts, and prompted them to imagine a more positive climate future, both locally and globally. Later, students formed groups and enacted speculative imagining to compose final project digital stories (Figure 1). We introduced this project at the beginning of our semester-long work with students. Subsequently, we engaged students in a series

Figure 1. PowerPoint slide introducing the final project

of speculative activities to scaffold their final project work.

Importantly, while the research team provided definitions for varying constructs such as civic engagement, speculation, and justice, we wanted students to express their understandings using their own words and examples. We reinforced this idea on a PowerPoint slide: "These terms can mean different things to different people and have impacts in different places." We completed a number of reflection prompts in which we invited students, who were seated in table groups to foster collaborative discussion, to write their own ideas down and then share them with their group peers. Student groups then shared out their diverse perspectives and understandings with peers.

Our Context: Seventh Grade Civics at Global Middle and High School

The work shared here comes from our instruction of two seventh-grade civics classes in the fall of 2023 at Global Middle and High School (GMHS), a public Title 1 charter school situated in a part of our city well known for its Cuban heritage. Almost all students in both class sections self-identified as immigrants or the children of immigrants and as bi/multilingual. These identifications are common for students in our majority-minority context in which nearly 60 percent of the city is foreign-born.

While our study was completed in a social studies department, we drew on a number of ELA approaches to support students' learning. This included introducing them to digital storytelling tools, engaging them in reflective writing, and supporting dialogic, peer, small-group, and whole-class sharing. Across the semester, students considered what it meant for them to be civically engaged, identified challenges they thought youth face in seeking to enact change based on how society positions them, and noted what approaches they might take to analyze existing systems and structures with the desire to transform our world. IRB permissions were given to conduct our study for purposes of research.

As referenced above, we introduced students to various inquiry approaches and digital storytelling tools promoting civic inquiry from past, present, and future perspectives. We focus our attention here on an activity in which students identified pressing issues or problems at GMHS and expressed their visions regarding how to create more just social futures at their school.

Scaffolding Understanding for Speculative Civic Imagining

To support students stepping into an imaginative space, we oriented one day of class instruction asking: *What might a more just future look like?* To start, we showed YouTube video clips of two youth community advocates: Mari Copeny, who addressed water quality in Flint, Michigan, and Luca Martinez, who advocated for wetland preservation in the Florida Everglades. Next, we provided students with a dictionary definition of the term "speculate." To make this term more applicable, one member of the research team equated the term "speculate" to "spectacles," inviting students to metaphorically put on glasses to envision better futures. Because we were aware of the challenges that come with imagining a world different from the one we currently live in, we prepared a slide (see Figure 2) with pictures of things that did not seem possible sixty years ago but are now a reality.

We scaffolded students' speculative imagining across multiple lessons using different

Figure 2. PowerPoint slide supporting speculative imagining

Figure 3. Student-generated sticky notes from "what if" and "why not" protocol

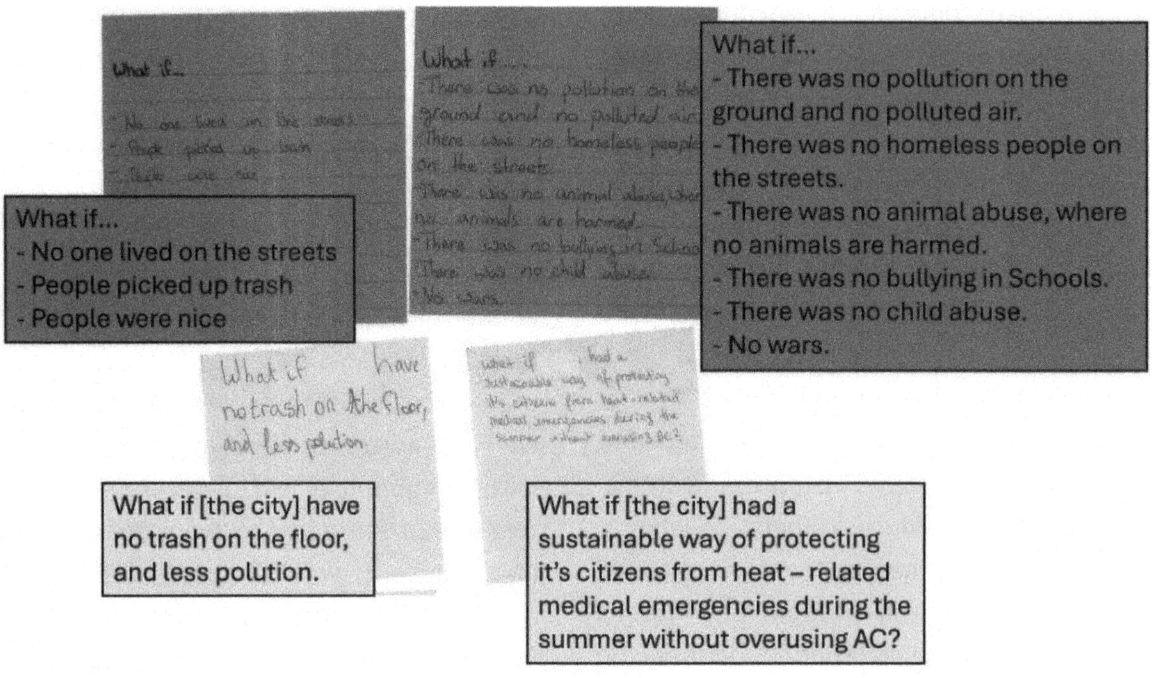

Researcher-created text boxes reflect students' writing

Table 1. Speculative activities

Lesson	Pedagogical Approaches	Speculative Activity(s)
Speculative Futures and Civic Engagement	Image analysis, individual brainstorming, class discussion	Define speculative/speculation, engage in class discussion of the terms via images and videos. Individual work creating and building a board of "what if" sticky notes (Figure 3). Whole-class discussion of student-generated concepts
Just Civic Futures	Scaffolded, handout-based at-home learning	Complete the scaffolded handout that leads students through imagining a more just future for their school (Figure 4)
Inquiry, Story telling, and PhotoVoice	Think-aloud, guided discussion, collaborative analysis, class discussion	Define inquiry, engage in class discussion of the terms via images and videos. Group analysis of PhotoVoice projects on civic issues
Storytelling and Inquiry via Oral Histories (family members)	Individual and collaborative video analysis, individual and collaborative brainstorming	Watch Henry Louis Gates interview about family histories. Student groups create a Past/Now/Future sticky-note note wall
Citizenship and Belonging & Workshop for Final Project	Group brainstorm, collaborative analysis, collaborative composition, collaborative digital image generation	Use graphic organizer to plan final projects that examine a locally important civic issue from Past/Present/Future perspectives. Create a Padlet highlighting speculative futures for a civic issue

pedagogical approaches and activities (Table 1). For example, to further help students address perceived constraints that come with imagining better futures, we took up Mirra and Garcia's (2023) "what if" and "why not" protocol. We asked: "What if healthy food was inexpensive?" "Why can't unhealthy food be expensive to buy?" We then invited students to write ideas on sticky notes, which they later affixed to the whiteboard for their peers to read (Figure 3).

We modeled for students how to address civic issues from both a past and present perspective before thinking about future changes. We focused on a student-generated civic concern: trash in the community. We guided students through a series of images and texts on a slideshow examining the trash issue locally (i.e., trash used to be stored outside of the community, but now the city has expanded, and some homes are now very close to a big landfill; we are running out of space to build new landfills). We also shared with students a news article highlighting how a local incinerator caught fire and was destroyed. We discussed the implications of the fire and its impact on the community (e.g., pollution; the need for a new way to dispose of trash).

Then we asked students to speculate: *How can we create a more socially responsible, just, and sustainable way of dealing with our trash?* Students used laptops to engage in research to find out more information about the topic and to look for current approaches that might lead to better futures. For example, one group discovered a startup company considering ways to mass produce packaging constructed from mushrooms. This group discussed how this type of packaging supported overall waste reduction, since the mushroom-based material was biodegradable. Following the in-class modeling explained above, students completed a graphic organizer in which they imagined (speculated) more just social futures at their school (see Figure 4).

The Focal Learning Task: Imagining (Speculating) a More Just Social Future at GMHS

We chose imagining more just social futures at GMHS because it was relevant to students, allowed them to extend and apply prior class learning, and supported them to engage in

Figure 4. Imagining (speculating) a more just social future at GMHS task

Imagine a more just social future at GMHS	What if . . .
What are challenges to making this imagination a reality?	
How could this imagination become reality? Share your ideas here	
How can these changes lead to a more just future for students at GMHS?	

Table 2. What ifs (imaginations)

Topic	# of Instances	Examples
Safety	8	Mike speculated: "What if at the end of periods, the hallways wouldn't be so tight"
Academic Support	3	Nathan speculated: [what if we] "Have more options than just PE and Robotics"
Well-Being	8	Laura speculated: [what if we] "Will have better healthier food"

imagining better civic futures, scaffolding their work for their culminating, digital storytelling project. To analyze their sharing, we inventoried their collective responses, setting up tables to look within and across their reporting to the four questions raised by the graphic organizer. Students who completed the assignment raised sixteen different issues, with three of those issues being identified by more than one student (i.e., healthier food in the cafeteria/providing free breakfast and lunch to students, wider hallways, and more places to store bicycles).

Findings: Students' Imaginations, Informed by Their Lived Experiences

Although asking students to address pressing issues at their school is not a novel one, asking them to be solution-oriented and future-focused was unique. This approach also reinforced students' critical and creative thinking skills. We organized students' concerns for issues at GMHS into three overarching categories: safety, academic support, and well-being (Table 2).

Students sought conditions leading to better schooling experiences and student success. In terms of safety, students wished there were bigger hallways with less crowding and pushing, a better space for parents dropping off and picking up their children, more parking for students and teachers driving to school, a place to secure bicycles, and cleaner restrooms. These concerns reflected the physical infrastructure limitations of the school: GMHS is located in a refurbished office building rented from a nearby business owner on one of our city's most famous streets. The space constraints further connected to students raised issues regarding academic support. Students noted GMHS lacks a library and offers limited class options and electives. Other concerns for well-being included: the desire that all students could get a passing score on state exams; later start times; healthier and free food served at the cafeteria; and that teachers and parents would listen to students' suggestions. Each issue, raised by students, mattered to them and, from our perspective, reflected their desire to engage in a civic-minded way to address challenges impacting their local school community.

To that end, in seeking to address these concerns, students were aware of barriers related to achieving better futures. For example, students wrote about limited resources like money to renovate the current school, add on to it, or build a new one. They further understood lack of access to quality products (e.g., healthier food) and services (e.g., space to expand parking) might further impede their aims for change. Some students were dismissive that others would not listen to them and their concerns because of their age, while others identified a lack of goodwill some individuals have toward change, even suggesting some people could never be convinced otherwise. Students further identified challenges of building consensus toward change and the higher costs that can come with doing what is right or good. Collectively, their responses demonstrated sophisticated understandings about civic change despite financial, attitudinal, or age-based obstacles.

In speculating for better futures, students addressed a number of actors and agents to support change. This aligned with prior scaffolding in which we asked students to identify individuals who could support their visions for civic advocacy, aligning to a state standard:

> SS.7.CG.2.10 Explain the process for citizens to address a state or local problem by researching public policy alternatives, identifying appropriate government agencies to address the issue and determining a course of action.

Specifically, students identified: talking with parents, appealing to adults employed by the school (janitors, teachers, administrators), meeting with school board members, seeking donations, and interacting with government officials for advocacy. However, this was hypothetical; students did not actually reach out to individuals for help with their concerns.

Students further examined how their proposed changes could lead to more just futures for students at GMHS. Their ideas about justice both written (as homework) and shared in class included removing current barriers to allow easier pathways for students' better futures, like opening up space to let "students do more things to learn" with less time spent on discipline or redirection and with everyone on track to pass the state test. Their just visions for the future also included helping students get to school "safer and easier and faster" due to more space to drop off and pick up, to park cars, and to secure bicycles. Students also saw increases in course offerings as justice-oriented with "more options/they can learn subjects that will benefit them in the future." They saw healthier, even free cafeteria food as relieving stress about affordability, giving them more energy, and supporting nutrition. They shared that this would help "to avoid such problems like (diabetes and other diseases linked to obesity)." Ultimately, students concluded their visions for more just social futures could lead to "students being happy in their student life."

Implications for Future Designs for Speculative Learning

Here, we discuss approaches for supporting students' speculative imagining and civic literacy practices in response to our project, which was completed in an urban, immigrant, and majority-minority school context.

The prompt for our activity—for students to reimagine their school experience—was not particularly complicated or challenging. We asked students to consider the changes they wanted to see at their school and the resulting ideas they came up with were complex and well developed. Our experiences suggest the types of topics or contexts to get students engaged in speculative imagining can be simple and familiar—and, we conjecture, the simpler and more familiar the context for imagining is, the richer students' engagement might be. However, as noted earlier, we hope that future designs provide more authentic outlets for sharing students' ideas and voices, whether that be within the school (i.e., establishing a presentation to school administrators and leading to actionable changes) or within their communities (i.e., inviting community leaders, advocates, or parents to have a conversation), which our project did not do.

That being said, we believe purposeful scaffolding may deepen students' speculative imagining skills. For instance, students were initially reluctant to take up the positive, agentic mindset that speculative imagining requires. In the standards-driven class where we engaged in research, pressing civic issues were not typically discussed, as the curricular focus was primarily on historical civic artifacts (i.e., Declaration of Independence, the US Constitution). When civic issues were introduced, students typically discussed these societal challenges as problems without solutions, perhaps mirroring arguments found in popular news or social media, but without engaging in further critique (see Mirra & Garcia, 2023, p. 78). Our instructional team did intentional work to have students practice imagining, to illustrate products of past imagining (e.g., Figure 2), and to frame students' day-to-day activities (e.g., selling candy bars to raise funds for student government; giving to charity; tutoring other students; intentionally recycling materials; giving food to the homeless) as participating in forms of local or community civic life. Students appreciated the opportunity to share "what could be" as a chance to provide "our own opinion and speculation on what was going to happen" (end-of-semester focus group). Nonetheless, some students still struggled to step into the speculative space, with one group reflecting "we don't know what the future is" (end-of-semester focus group).

Our particular adaptation of Mirra and Garcia's (2023) framework helped us emphasize the historical continuum of civic issues (past, present, and future) as part of civic world building. In our end-of-semester group interviews, students reported difficulties in understanding their identified civic issues in the past or as historically situated. As such, our study suggests the importance of supporting students for making deeper connections to civic issues historically. This may include introducing tools to engage students in historical research and develop their skills in writing and framing issues from the past. Other research designs have explored innovative digital literacies-learning environments for historical investigations (e.g., Hall et al., 2020); future work could strengthen this inquiry piece by incorporating other design features.

We also found students who drew on their lived experiences had less trouble understanding issues in the present. For example, students' oral history interviews with family members supported localized knowledge as informed by their family's past migration experiences, reflecting students' identities in our majority-minority context (see also, Deroo et al., 2024).

Finally, our work with students demonstrated speculative world building's potential to align to standards even in state contexts that have a high level of governmental curricular oversight regarding permissible topics for instruction. While our study took place in a seventh-grade civics classroom and aligned with social studies frameworks, our work was interdisciplinary and could easily be aligned to our state's seventh-grade ELA standards, such as those around argument and argumentative writing; researching and critically using information; leveraging multimedia for storytelling; and providing additional social and historical context for fiction and nonfiction literary texts. Students practiced supporting claims using evidence from sources; acknowledging counter-perspectives to arguments; and calling upon multiple valid and reliable sources to support claims. In our digital storytelling activities, students integrated audio, video, pictures, and/or digital resources into their artifacts. Our experiences thus suggest that speculative activities can be aligned successfully with mandated curricula. Furthermore, we see the alignment with standards as important for being responsive to laws that seek to limit certain topics and discussions. To that end, by allowing students to take the lead in sharing their perspectives in all inquiry and conversation, we were able to enact speculative activities within state-oriented constraints.

Conclusion

We presented our experiences with implementing a speculative learning design in a seventh-grade civics class. Our research responded to Mirra and Garcia's (2023) call to honor youth voices and perspectives. In our classrooms, we positioned youth, who are often marginalized in civic spaces given their age and their racial and linguistic identities, as authority figures for their futures. We hope that others will continue this work in both civics and ELA spaces, as we see speculative civics practices as interdisciplinary and supportive of disciplinary learning goals. For practitioners, first steps toward adopting a speculative framework might look like encouraging students to imaginatively reflect on a topic or issue. For researchers, we encourage them to investigate other ELA pedagogical approaches that take up speculative approaches. We trust the work featured here might become increasingly common, one in which all students have the opportunity to speculate for more just civic futures for themselves and for their communities.

Works Cited

Banks, J. A. (2017). Failed citizenship and transformative civic education. *Educational Researcher, 46*(7), 366–377.

Deroo, M. R., Kahn, J., & Axelrod, D. (2024). Leveraging linguistic and cultural frames for social-spatial understandings with transnational youth. In A. Jaffe and C. Salinas (Eds.) *Teaching culturally and linguistically relevant social studies with and for emergent bilingual and multilingual youth: Examining the past, present, and future* (pp. 34–50). Teacher's College Press.

Duncan, K. (Ed.). (2023). *Civic engagement in communities of color: Pedagogy for learning and life in a more expansive democracy.* Teachers College Press.

Garcia, A., & Morrell, E. (2022). *Tuned-in teaching: Centering youth culture for an active and just classroom.* Heinemann.

Hall, R., Shapiro, B. R., Hostetler, A., Lubbock, H., Owens, D., Daw, C., & Fisher, D. (2020). Here-and-then: Learning by making places with digital spatial story lines. *Cognition and Instruction, 38*(3), 348–373.

Kahn, J., Axelrod, D, Deroo, M. R., Radojcic, S. (2022). Stories from Islita Libre: Digital spatial storytelling as an expression of transnational and immigrant identities. Bank Street Occasional Series (48), 96–112.

Lyiscott, J., Mirra, N., & Garcia, A. (2021). *Critical media literacy and popular culture in ELA classrooms.* National Council of Teachers of English. https://ncte.org/wp-content/uploads/2021/04/SquireOfficePolicyBrief_CriticalMediaLiteracy_April2021.pdf

Mirra, N., & Garcia, A. (2022). Guns, schools, and democracy: Adolescents imagining social futures through speculative civic literacies. *American Educational Research Journal, 59*(2), 345–380.

Mirra, N., & Garcia, A. (2023). *Civics for the world to come: Committing to democracy in every classroom.* W. W. Norton & Company.

Rubin, B., & Hayes, B. (2010). "No backpacks" versus "drugs and murder": The promise and complexity of youth civic action research. *Harvard Educational Review, 80*(3), 352–378.

Sinclair, K. A., Rodriguez, S., & Monreal, T. P. (2023). "We can be leaders": Minoritized youths' subjugated (civic) knowledges and social futures in two urban contexts. *International Journal of Qualitative Studies in Education, 36*(3), 392–410.

Westheimer, J., & Kahne, J. (2004). Educating the "good" citizen: Political choices and pedagogical goals. *PS: Political Science & Politics, 37*(2), 241–247.

Wray-Lake, L., & Abrams, L. S. (2020). Pathways to civic engagement among urban youth of color. *Monographs of the Society for Research in Child Development, 85*(2), 7–154.

SECTION 2
Supporting Black Students' Civic Engagement from Kinder through College

Researching Black Girl Literacy Practices in Predominantly White Schools: An Archaeology of the Self

TYANA VELAZQUEZ-SMITH

Introduction

As I sat with eleven girls in grades K–3 in a predominantly white elementary school where only 2 percent of the student population was Black girls, the sentiments they shared echoed in my ears. They described feeling "ugly," "not like the rest," not good enough, and not having "white girl hair." The girls discussed how their teacher treated them differently than white students and how their white peers taunted them. These experiences mirrored my own memories as a Black girl in a predominantly white school—being taunted for "being left in the oven too long" and being called the N-word. The pain and exclusion these young girls felt were all too familiar to me.

In researching their literacy practices, I embarked on what Dr. Yolanda Sealey-Ruiz (2021) describes as "an archaeology of the self," a process of critically examining how race and racism shape our personal and professional lives. This phenomenological study, rooted in grounded theory, interprets findings through critical race theory (CRT) and Black Feminist Thought (BFT), which explore the intersectionality of race, gender, and social categorizations and their societal implications.

As a Black autistic woman, I confront the daily intersections of racism, sexism, and ableism. This research has deepened my engagement with these oppressive forces while also prompting a journey toward self-healing. By integrating personal reflections with critical race and intersectional analysis, this study highlights the transformative power of embracing lived experiences as a key element of scholarly inquiry.

The research took place across six classrooms: one kindergarten, two first grade, two second grade, and one third grade. It involved interviews with parents/caregivers, focus groups, and classroom observations, focusing on the lived experiences of Black girls in a predominantly white elementary school and their literacy practices during ELA time. Interviews were held in a separate room to create a safer space, apart from the white gaze, allowing for more authentic expressions of their experiences.

Cultural Intuition as a Compass

Early in the data collection phase, I realized that my personal healing as a traumatized Black girl was incomplete. This ongoing healing journey became a compass throughout the research process. To conduct this study effectively, I needed to release the "dirty pain"—a term Dr. Resmaa Menakem uses to describe pain tied to avoidance, blame, and denial (Menakem, 2017). Failure to confront this pain led to a mental health crisis three weeks into data collection. To address this, I embraced cultural intuition—a methodological approach introduced by Delgado Bernal (1998) and rooted in Chicana feminist epistemologies. This approach transformed my research into an act of resistance and revolutionized my perspective, using my healing to amplify my voice and the often-silenced voices of these girls. Cultural intuition became a healing modality, allowing me to reclaim my body from the influence of white supremacy and violence.

Together with the participants, our space-taking—formed through cultural intuition—emerged as a cultural literary practice. This practice encompasses the ways cultural groups share and create meaning. No group laughs harder or tells their life stories with more richness than Black girls.

The Materialization of White Supremacy

White supremacy profoundly shapes the experiences of Black girls in predominantly white schools. This research, based on classroom observations, literacy artifact analysis, and interviews with students, parents, and teachers, uncovered seven critical themes illustrating the systemic obstacles these students face. It reveals not only overt racial tensions but also the subtle, yet equally harmful, manifestations of systemic racism embedded in school cultures.

Nine of the eleven girls reported emotionally, physically, and psychologically aggressive interactions with white peers, exacerbated by the school's inadequate antiracist measures. Ten participants recounted harmful interactions with white teachers, highlighting the systemic failure to address racism in teacher-student dynamics. Many students reported feelings of isolation and exclusion, contrasting with the school's professed values of inclusivity. This sense of alienation was compounded by internalized racism, affecting eight participants and diminishing their self-esteem. Some girls even disclosed struggles with mental health, including suicidal thoughts, underscoring the intense pressures they faced.

The curriculum posed further challenges by often failing to acknowledge Black histories and contributions beyond tokenistic mentions during Black History Month. This left students feeling further marginalized. Despite a general affinity for literacy, participants found the English language arts (ELA) curriculum uninspiring and unstimulating, highlighting a need for reform to better engage and nurture these girls.

The findings of this study were enriched by the participants' use of literacy as a form of expression. In focus groups and interviews, their thoughtful use of language allowed them to articulate their experiences and resist marginalization. These narratives were not simply recounted; they were actively constructed through their interactions with texts, asserting their agency and creativity.

Anti-Black Self-Conceptualizations

White supremacy deeply impacts the psyche of Black girls, convincing them they are simultaneously not enough, too much, and too little. This was evident during the research. In one focus group, participants described feeling "ugly," "not like the rest," or having "bad hair." These internalized sentiments highlight the deep-seated issues stemming from systemic racism and normalized white violence.

In a one-on-one interview, while coloring dolls with a first-grade participant, I colored my doll brown, and she colored hers peach. Guided by my cultural intuition, I asked which doll she thought was prettier. Recalling my own childhood preference for the peach crayon, I hoped her answer would differ. However, she pointed to the peach-colored doll and stated, "Brown skin is disgusting. I don't like my skin color. I only like my eye color. I like my brown eyes but not my skin brown." When I asked if she found my skin disgusting, her affirmative answer twisted my stomach—a familiar feeling for those of us taught to despise our skin. Rather than challenging her immediate perception, I asked about the origins of her views. She explained that she was the only Black girl in her class and the only one who didn't receive "Paw Bucks"—the school's behavior incentive system.

This child drew parallels between her exclusion and her brown skin, seeing the peach doll as safer, not necessarily prettier. Scholars like Martha Nussbaum (2004) discuss how the politics of disgust marginalize people and reinforce social hierarchies. Because of her experiences, the Black girl viewed the peach doll as safer.

In her eyes, the peach doll, symbolizing whiteness, exists safely within a system designed to protect her, while the brown doll, representing Blackness, is seen as perpetually at risk. This understanding of safety transcends beauty, reflecting her awareness of racial dynamics even at a young age.

Loneliness and Exclusion

Educational settings often serve as platforms where systemic biases promote a preference for whiteness, influencing young minds through a curriculum that marginalizes other identities. This bias was evident in the literacy artifacts from my study, particularly with a second-grade participant. Overwhelmed by exclusion, she used a drawing to express her discomfort. Her artwork declared, "Not everything can be white," challenging the dominance of white characters in her classroom library. This statement and her desire to write books featuring Black characters were not just a wish but a profound critique of the racial erasure in her educational environment.

Figure 1

The narrative "I am here; why can't you see me?" emerged during our discussions, highlighting the isolation Black students often feel in predominantly white schools. This young scholar's question reflects the normalization of whiteness that pervades her daily experiences. Her choice of the book title *I Am Beautiful* serves as a counter-narrative to the marginalization she encounters.

When I asked her to elaborate on her feelings, a question informed by my own experiences as a Black girl, she replied: "It's frustrating because I am here; why can't you [the school] see that I am here?" (Angela, field notes, March 24, 2022). This dialogue illustrates the profound impact of systemic neglect on Black students' recognition and emotional health within educational systems shaped by whiteness.

Her creation of the title *I Am Beautiful* is a rejection of the systemic "othering" she faces, asserting her identity and worth in a space that often ignores both. Naming herself in the narrative directly challenges the dominant cultural narratives that marginalize her identity in her educational context.

Figure 2

Suicidality and Racial Trauma

As I walked through the halls of Eagle Elementary, the setting felt all too familiar—an echo of my experiences in a predominantly white school during childhood. The environment wasn't overtly hostile, but the racial tension mirrored the emotional violence I had endured. This atmosphere of defensiveness and exclusion required the adoption of a protective guise, much like in my own elementary school. Barely three weeks into the study, a petition by the staff to remove me from classrooms marked me as an unwelcome intruder, reflecting prejudices rather than any real threat posed by my presence or research (Researcher journal, April 5, 2022).

An incident unfolded when a teacher's seemingly benign inquiry revealed deep-seated racial prejudices. She tried to compare slurs directed at Italian individuals to the pervasive violence Black individuals face. Recounting a childhood story, she casually said, "I was so 'Black' they even called me a (racial slur)." Her nonchalant use of the N-word left me shocked and disoriented. As she noticed my reaction, she asked, "Oh, did I offend you? I was only trying to illustrate that Italian children also face racial violence in school" (Researcher journal, March 15, 2022). Her final question, "Did I say something that offended you?" shifted the burden onto me, exemplifying how victims are often forced to justify their pain—an abuse of power dynamics.

This interaction revealed the systemic issues students like Araminta, a young Black girl in the study, experienced. After being racially abused by a peer, Araminta was disciplined instead of supported. During her in-school suspension, she created a distressing artwork titled "Kill Myself," in which she depicted herself in an orange jumpsuit, symbolizing her feeling of imprisonment. Araminta's words—"That's the title because when I get in trouble, I think of suicide a lot because when I am at this school, I want to leave this earth"—painfully encapsulate the psychological impact of the hostile school climate. Her experience exemplifies the broader failures that perpetuate trauma among Black students.

This environment not only amplified my past traumas but also triggered suicidal thoughts. By the third month of my research, the weight of revisiting these oppressive dynamics became overwhelming. As I wrote in my journal on February 27, 2022:

> Today I left my house and looked at my husband like it was the last time I would see him. I feel like I am losing pieces of myself daily, and every day on my way to school, I think about taking my life. I almost didn't make it today because I wanted everything to end, and every day the urge gets stronger. I took longer to leave this morning, not sure if my eyes said anything, but if they did, they would have said I love you and

Figure 3

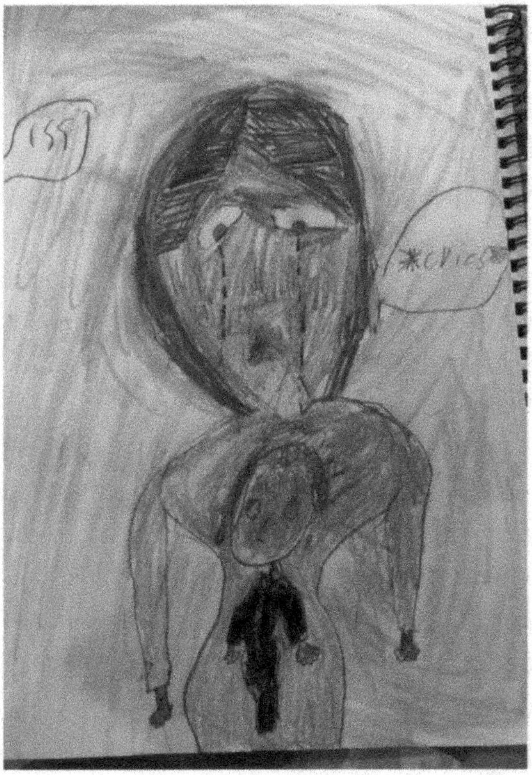

> I'm sorry. I'm in the parking lot, shocked I made it because the whole drive I was figuring out how to end my life without harming others. I'm scared because I have little control, and something strong has taken over me. Nothing is working—not therapy, breaks, or talking—and I feel like my humanness is slipping away. My plan to get better isn't working, and I am broken. I need help but feel I can't ask for it.

This personal crisis echoes the despair felt by participants like Araminta, underscoring the profound toll systemic racism and educational neglect take on mental health. These narratives are not just academic; they reflect the lived experiences of Black girls and women, highlighting the urgent need for systemic change. Acknowledging and addressing the deep-seated racism that shapes countless Black students' educational experiences is the first step. Through cultural intuition, this study documented these injustices and fostered a deeper connection with participants, creating a shared space for understanding and healing.

Navigating Invisibility

During my time at Eagle Elementary, the sentiments expressed by participants triggered a personal memory, deepening my understanding of the invisibility and exclusion Black girls experience in predominantly white schools. I vividly recalled a day from my own childhood when I felt invisible. This belief was so entrenched that during a casual outing to the grocery store with my father, I was shocked when a classmate acknowledged me with a wave. The shock of being seen after feeling consistently unseen was visceral—a reminder of the isolation I felt in school. This childhood experience resonated with the stories voiced by the participants at Eagle Elementary.

One participant, Kayla, embodied themes of exclusion and a longing for escape through her creation of a "raft," adorned with art supplies and labeled "Kayla's Raft." When asked about its purpose, she replied, "It's to get the heck out of here. I am tired of it here in this classroom, so I am building a raft to sail away" (Kayla, field notes, March 29, 2022). She added that she planned to bring other Black girls with her, revealing that it wasn't just a personal escape but a collective liberation—a journey to a sanctuary they could call their own.

The sense of community and support among the girls was exemplified in their other literacy activities, such as bracelet making. These bracelets, inscribed with affirmations like "BFF," "Black girl magic," and "Black girls are pretty," were exchanged as gifts, affirming each other's worth and beauty.

During these sessions, rich conversations unfolded, filled with shared experiences. Marian, while crafting a bracelet for Nilah, expressed, "In my class, I always work alone, but I think I prefer to be with you all because everyone is white, and it's nice to do writing and playing with you all" (Focus group interview 1). This acknowledgment of their collective experience, in contrast to the alienation they felt in regular classes, highlighted the importance of these spaces of solidarity.

In a particularly poignant demonstration of support, when Araminta faced a three-day suspension for defending herself against a racist attack by a white peer, Nilah crafted a card filled with positive affirmations. This gesture was more than kindness; it was a powerful declaration of Araminta's worth: "There is nothing bad about you." This reassurance was crucial, reminding Araminta that despite the punitive measures, she remained valued, loved, and important. These acts of solidarity reflect the enduring resilience and unity among Black women throughout history. When Angela Davis was unjustly imprisoned, Black women rallied for her freedom. When Zora Neale Hurston's contributions risked obscurity, Alice Walker revived her legacy. In the wake of tragedies like Sandra Bland and Breonna Taylor, the collective outcry ensured their stories were not forgotten.

The young participants in this study, through their shared literary expressions, embody this legacy. Their solidarity and creative expressions are not mere activities; they are manifestations of a profound archaeology of the self that both reveals and heals. By connecting their present actions with the historical resilience of Black women, they deepen their understanding of their experiences, helping them navigate their present with a strong sense of identity and support.

Analyzing Violent Interactions and Identity Affirmation

Reflecting on my own experiences as a Black girl in predominantly white schools deeply informs the perspective I bring to this study. Painful memories of exclusion, racial comments from teachers, and aggressive peer interactions—such as being told I had been "left in the oven too long," having a kindergarten teacher admit she had never taught a Black child before, and being called the N-word, which resulted in my suspension while the aggressor was unpunished—mirror the violent interactions faced by the participants. These incidents, defined here as violence, encompass any actions that cause physical, emotional, or psychological harm, representing a broad range of damaging interactions.

A poignant example is Norma's recounting of a racially charged playground game at her kindergarten. In this game, white students chased and "enslaved" Brown students. While framed as innocuous play by her peers, it was, in reality, a powerful enactment of white supremacy—a literal chasing down of Black bodies by white ones.

Norma's teacher's response when she bravely voiced her concerns is emblematic of the systemic silencing Black individuals often face. By dismissing her concerns as "creative imagination" and advising skepticism, the teacher invalidated Norma's distress and upheld a narrative that protects the status quo while disregarding the violence of such a game.

This incident exemplifies how Black children are subjected to racial oppression, often normalized or dismissed by authority figures. These experiences profoundly impact self-perception, with Norma expressing a wish to be white to escape the fear and injustice she associates with being on the "brown team." This reflects the internalized racial inferiority that oppressive systems instill in Black individuals from a young age.

Conclusion

The journey of exploring the literacy practices of eleven girls in a predominantly white school through the lens of cultural intuition has been both painful and transformative. The narratives of collective identity, resistance, and cultural intuition in this study challenge the invisibility Black girls face. By connecting their present actions with historical literacy practices of Black women, they deepen their understanding of their experiences, empowering them to navigate educational spaces with a stronger sense of identity and support.

Reflecting on these experiences, it is clear that cultural intuition serves as a compass for Black women researchers. It allows us to confront and heal from the traumas of systemic racism and sexism. Embracing lived experiences as a critical component of scholarly inquiry not only validates our voices but also transforms research into acts of resistance and healing.

In this spirit, I share my own literacy practice—a poem that speaks to the resilience and strength of Black girls. It is a reminder that despite the violence and challenges we face, we possess an inherent power and beauty that cannot be diminished.

> Dear Black girl,
> They tell you who you are.
> Then say you won't go far.
> Black girl, they take away your style.
> Then tell you to smile.
> Black girl, they hush you in a crowd.
> Then chastise you for being too loud.
> Black girl, the wind could be at your back.
> And on the news, we'd hear that you staged the attack.
> Black girl, they will tear off your wings and watch you fall.
> And then, Black girl, they will blame you for it all.
> Black girl, they will scar your name.
> They will tell you that you created your pain.
> But you listen to me, my love.
> You are delicate and soft.
> Because you are cut from the finest cloth.
> Black girl, you see, the world wants you.
> Every part.
> For your mind, spirit, body, and heart.
> But they can't have your special parts.
> Despite their rotten history of the things, they say and do.
> So, these words are for you.
> Spread your wings and take it high.
> Take those wings, and I'll watch you fly.
> Because like Toni said, you are your best thing.
> And your essence, Black girl, will forever sing.

Afterword: Implications for Civic Learning and Educational Practice

Given this volume's focus on K–12 classroom practices and civic engagement, this essay underscores how literacy practices can serve as powerful tools for both personal and communal transformation. The narratives of the girls, their struggles, and their acts of solidarity highlight the necessity of creating educational spaces that acknowledge and actively combat systemic racism.

This essay addresses the educational spaces that adhere to white supremacy culture and undermine girls' abilities to thrive. It presents to practitioners the harm they may unknowingly perpetuate and offers critical reflection on the necessary steps to foster more inclusive and supportive learning environments.

To align with the volume's theme, the following steps focus on advancing civic learning and promoting systemic change:

1. **Abolish Racist Policies and Practices:** Schools must actively work to identify and dismantle policies and practices that perpetuate racism and inequality. This includes reevaluating disciplinary measures, dress codes, and curriculum standards that disproportionately affect Black students.

2. **Foster Radical Inclusivity:** Create educational spaces that not only include but celebrate the identities and cultures of all students. This involves integrating culturally sustaining pedagogy and practices into every aspect of the school environment, promoting a sense of belonging and respect for diversity.
3. **Implement Restorative Justice Practices:** Move away from punitive disciplinary measures toward restorative justice practices that emphasize healing and community building. This approach addresses the root causes of conflicts and supports the emotional and psychological well-being of all students.
4. **Engage in Continuous Reflection and Accountability:** Educators and administrators must engage in ongoing self-reflection and hold themselves accountable for their actions and the impact they have on students. This includes regular training on antiracism, antibias, and cultural competency, fostering a commitment to equity and justice.
5. **Promote Community and Parental Involvement:** Actively involve parents and the broader community in the educational process. Strengthening the support network for students ensures that diverse perspectives are included in decision-making processes and that educational practices reflect the needs and values of the community.
6. **Invest in Mental Health Resources:** Ensure that mental health resources are accessible and culturally responsive. Recognizing the unique challenges faced by students of color and providing appropriate support is crucial for their well-being and academic success.

By implementing these steps, learning spaces and educators can create a transformative vision of civic learning grounded in equity, justice, and cultural responsiveness. Civic learning, as defined within the Black community, involves fostering critical consciousness, community engagement, and a commitment to social justice (Ginwright, 2010). This vision not only challenges the systemic barriers faced by Black girls but also enriches the educational experience for all students. The practice of cultural intuition, or archaeology of the self, becomes a civic act—where understanding and valuing one's identity and experiences empowers students to engage critically and compassionately with their communities. Through this commitment to radical inclusivity and restorative practices, we can cultivate educational spaces that honor the dignity and potential of every student, fostering a society where justice and equity are the foundations of civic learning.

Works Cited

Bernal, D. D. (1998). Using a Chicana feminist epistemology in educational research. *Harvard Educational Review, 68(*4), 555–583.

Ginwright, S. (2010). *Black youth rising: Activism and radical healing in urban America.* Teachers College Press.

Menakem, R. (2017). *My grandmother's hands: Racialized trauma and the pathway to mending our hearts and bodies.* Central Recovery Press.

Nussbaum, M. C. (2004). *Hiding from humanity: Disgust, shame, and the law.* Princeton University Press.

Sealey-Ruiz, Y. (2021). *The Archeology of the Self: A framework for teaching and learning to undress racism.* Teachers College Press.

"I'm a teacher and I cannot talk about those things": Reimagining Civics Education through the Perspectives of Adolescent Black Girls

LAKISHA ODLUM

> *So, civics for dark folx is our life . . . but nothing can ever measure how dark people fight injustice, find ways to love, and build community, which makes being a dark person a civics project.*
>
> —Bettina L. Love

Introduction

During the 2024 presidential campaign, former President Donald J. Trump gave a speech to a group of his supporters in which he promised that if elected, "We're going to give our police their power back, and we're going to give them immunity from prosecution, so they're not prosecuted for doing their job." While Trump's statement was met with applause from his supporters, the response from Black people on social media was one of disgust and fear. Trump's comment comes after years-long efforts to limit and abolish qualified immunity for police officers in myriad states and cities (Legal Defense Fund, 2024). Hearing Trump's speech was triggering for me, and the image of former Minneapolis police officer Derek Chauvin's knee on George Floyd's neck in 2020 flashed in my mind. I shuddered thinking about the possible implications on the Black community of Trump's agenda, and I remembered how the murders of George Floyd and Breonna Taylor impacted my Black students at that time.

Although many schools and districts acknowledged that the Black Lives Matter movement of 2020 was an opportunity to have important conversations about racism and civic engagement (Barnum & Belsha, 2020), many were ill-prepared to address the trauma that Black students faced. Consequently, the social and emotional needs of Black students who were living through "twin pandemics"—COVID-19 and anti-Black racism—were neglected, and non-Black students weren't provided with critical ways to evaluate and process the trauma that they repeatedly saw in the media.

In "Let's Go There: Making a Case for Race, Ethnicity and a Lived Civics Approach to Civic Education," Cohen et al. (2018) assert that

> While young people of color are raising their voices, getting involved with groups in their communities, and taking to the streets to advance a political agenda meant to address and improve their lives, it is not clear that current approaches to teaching civics in urban classrooms adequately or effectively center or engage these same young people. (p. 3)

As Cohen et al. state, students of color are civically engaged in their communities; however, schools are not tapping into the civic literacies they espouse outside of school. In this essay, I argue that in order for English educators to effectively incorporate civics education into the classroom, students' voices must be at the center. The "banking model" (Freire, 1970) of civics education will not suffice in our current political climate. It is imperative that teachers listen to the needs and concerns of their students and become co-constructors of knowledge with them. Moreover, as Dr. Bettina L. Love (2019) asserts in the epigraph of this chapter, Black people have a unique relationship with civics, and the Black perspective on civics education is critical in developing twenty-first century civics curricula. As such, this essay draws on my own research that centers the voices of adolescent Black girls whom I interviewed in 2020 during the COVID-19 pandemic. I center Black girls in my work because their voices are often excluded from conversations about curriculum, social justice, and racism. Their wisdom and insights about how their schools responded to the murders of Breonna Taylor and George Floyd, as well as the ways their secondary English teachers approached conversations about race and social justice, offer us guidance on how schools and secondary English teachers can reimagine their approach to civics education.

Research Context

During the COVID-19 school shutdowns of 2020, I conducted Zoom interviews with six adolescent Black girls about the ways their schools addressed the murders of Breonna Taylor and George Floyd. I espoused the Black Girls' Literacies framework (Muhammad & Haddix, 2016; Sealey-Ruiz, 2016; Price-Dennis, 2016) and intersectionality (Crenshaw, 1989) as a way to center and understand the experiences of adolescent Black girls. All of the young women were high school students when the school shutdowns occurred. I refer to these young women as Crystal, Bella, Raven, Stacey, Natasha, and Monique. The guiding question for this essay is: *How can secondary English teachers create a classroom environment that respects the lived experiences of Black students and fosters civic engagement?* In the subsequent sections, I delineate and analyze the young women's responses to the interview questions and offer some ways secondary English teachers can cultivate a culture of civic engagement by centering race and social justice in their classrooms.

How Schools Addressed the Murders of Breonna Taylor and George Floyd

In order to gain an understanding of the different ways secondary schools addressed the murders of Breonna Taylor, George Floyd, and the Black Lives Matter protests, I asked the young women the following questions: *1) Was the murder of George Floyd/Breonna Taylor and/or the protests addressed by your school? 2) How did they address the issues? 3) Were you satisfied or dissatisfied with the way your school addressed these issues?* Their responses were as follows:

> ***Monique:*** *It was addressed, but it was only addressed after we had to say something. I went to a predominantly white school, and all of the Black students who were there realized that a couple of days went by, and nobody was talking about it. So, we actually had to band together to make them aware that this was happening and that they should be saying something.*
>
> *I wasn't satisfied with how they handled or addressed it, but it did start a lot of conver-*

sation. And so, I'm glad that we got to that point, but I feel like the school could have handled it better and earlier than they did.

Raven: *Yeah, there was an email talking about that. They don't agree with what happened, and they post on their Instagram ways to petition, charities to donate to, and things like that.*

I was satisfied because I would say there wasn't much that they could do.

Stacey: *My school did not. They mostly just gave out Google Forms. It was mostly if the teachers felt like they wanted to.*

I was definitely dissatisfied because when something major comes out, they don't talk about it or they sweep it under the rug, so all the white people could feel better about themselves, so the parents don't have a problem.

Natasha: *It was an email, and they were saying how [Black people] were being treated and . . . they were just telling us to be safe.*

I was satisfied because oftentimes you don't really expect the school to say much about that. I was surprised because my school is not only Black people.

Bella: *No. There's a rule at my school that you can't really get into politics and beliefs and stuff, so nobody really addressed it.*

I was pretty dissatisfied. The majority of the population is Black or minorities, so yeah, I do wish that they addressed it.

Crystal: *Not really. My school put out a statement about it, but that was about it.*

I was very dissatisfied. The school not addressing it led to a lot of anger within our school. Not only did my school ignore it, but a lot of the world ignored Breonna Taylor as well. And I feel like that's the sad reality for Black women in America today.

The young women's responses revealed that there was no substantial effort on the part of any of their schools to address the murders of Breonna Taylor and George Floyd nor to address the Black Lives Matter protests. General statements were made, obligatory Google Forms were sent out, and in Monique's case, the school only organized an assembly after students confronted administrators about the lack of attention to the issue. Raven's school was somewhat of an outlier because they shared ways to get involved on the school's social media accounts, but they did not organize any schoolwide or classroom conversations. The young women's statements about their satisfactions and dissatisfactions revealed two things: First, the young women who were satisfied had low expectations for their schools to begin with, so the fact that their schools made some effort was sufficient for them. Second, the young women who were dissatisfied believed that their school administrators valued the feelings and comfort of white students and families more than the impact of the racial trauma on their Black students.

In "Choosing to See the Racial Stress That Afflicts Our Black Students," Anderson et al. (2019) explained the necessity of schools supporting Black students through racial trauma and delineated the myriad side effects young Black people face as a result of racial trauma:

> For Black youth in particular, the negative physical, psychological, physiological, and academic effects of racism include traumatic symptoms (e.g., hyper-vigilance about potential acts of racism), diminished self-esteem, symptoms of depression, impaired academic self-concepts, decreased school engagement, and lower academic performance, to name a few. (p. 22)

Black students in the United States are suffering from the impact of systemic racism, yet schools consistently fail to acknowledge its severe side effects. Moreover, when schools aren't involved, Black parents and guardians bear the full burden of helping their children process racial trauma while they themselves are suffering through their own racial trauma (Anderson et al., 2019). In order for schools to be spaces in which civic engagement is developed and nurtured, school leaders have to strategically, critically, and empathetically address the racial harm that is experienced by Black people in the United States.

How Teachers Address Racism in the Secondary English Classroom

The secondary English classroom is often stereotyped as a therapeutic, utopian space in which students engage in reading, writing, and discussions about the world and are able to process their feelings with the support of their peers and teachers. While that is what many of us strive for, it is often not the reality. I wanted to gain an understanding of the young women's experiences with having conversations about racism and social justice in the English classroom; therefore, I asked them: *Have you ever talked about racism or social justice in the English classroom (middle/high school)?* They responded as follows:

> ***Raven:*** *We would read about books where somebody, because of their skin color or religion, would be discriminated against.*
>
> ***Stacey:*** *I did bring up racism in English class . . . Both of my teachers definitely do feel uncomfortable when someone brings up racism and definitely do start the conversation with "I'm a teacher and I cannot talk about those things. . . ." They do not want to make white people uncomfortable.*
>
> ***Natasha:*** *We read* Homegoing *by Yaa Gyasi . . . . We mainly talked about how slaves were being treated and what the owners would do to them.*
>
> ***Bella:*** *We talked about racism with* To Kill a Mockingbird.
>
> ***Crystal:*** *From middle school to high school, I feel like none of my English classes have ever acknowledged what has gone on in the world. I think my English classes were mainly focused on the curriculum. If we were talking about racism or feminism or sexism, it really had to be circulated around the book.*

Conversations about racism and social justice issues were not a consistent practice in the English classrooms in which the young women were students. When the topics were discussed, they were always connected to a whole-class text as opposed to a response to current events. Stacey believed that her teachers never facilitated these discussions because they did not want to offend the white students. She also said that her teachers explicitly stated that they were not "allowed" to have conversations about race and social justice with students. In *Civics for the World to Come: Committing to Democracy in Every Classroom*, Mirra and Garcia (2023) address the idea of political neutrality in the classroom and contend that the act of not talking about political issues is political in and of itself:

> This is why we say neutrality is impossible in the classroom and there is no option of sitting on the sidelines. Even if we vowed to avoid all talk of the world beyond the four walls of our classrooms and follow our district's mandated curriculum to the letter, we would through these acts still be expressing political values. (p. 10–11)

The repercussions of having conversations about racism and social justice are real, especially in our current political climate of book bans, mandates for Christian education in public schools, and Project 2025; however, to avoid the conversations altogether only further inflicts harm on our most vulnerable students and conveys the message that we do not care for their well-being. Furthermore, students cannot become "competent and responsible citizens" if they never have the opportunity to discuss these societal issues in class. As Meira Levinson (2010) asserts, "Competent and responsible citizens . . . have an understanding and awareness of public and community issues; and have the ability to obtain information, think critically, and enter into dialogue among others with different perspectives" (p. 317). If "all teachers are civics teachers" (Mirra & Garcia, 2023), it is imperative that secondary English teachers adequately prepare their students for democratic citizenship by engaging in critical dialogue with their students.

How Secondary English Teachers Can Support Black Students

As a teacher educator, researcher, and former secondary English teacher, centering the voices and literacies of my students has always been a primary value; therefore, it was important for me to hear the young women's thoughts on how they would like English teachers to support Black students. Their responses were realistic, powerful, and easy to accomplish:

> ***Monique:*** *I think that bringing in real-world experiences and really talking about issues that are happening in the world and tying in their own experiences to different topics and having a place where you could really talk about that would be very beneficial.*
>
> ***Raven:*** *Trying to just understand our feelings and observing what's happening in society and bringing it into class.*
>
> ***Stacey:*** *They definitely should let us talk about [race] just like how the white people get to . . . . They definitely should let Black women talk about the issues that they go through not just for five minutes, we definitely should have more Black women come up and speak to the class. We definitely should incorporate Black women into everyday things that we do because we are in everyday things that people do.*
>
> ***Natasha:*** *I feel like making us do group projects and researching [Black] people or giving us a book to read about a Black person.*
>
> ***Bella:*** *I guess just acknowledging what's going on in terms of Black Lives Matter. I guess being in support of Black Lives Matter.*

> ***Crystal:*** *I think just making the space—not ignoring the things that are going on in our world because there are so many ways to tie a text into the thing that we're going through currently. Because books and novels and magazines, anything really, is drawn—any art is drawn from our experiences and what we have gone through and what's going on now.*

The young women's responses reaffirm what the research on culturally relevant pedagogy (Ladson-Billings, 2013) and culturally and historically responsive education (CHRE) (Muhammad, 2020) have taught us: 1) Black students want their teachers to explicitly acknowledge the injustices that plague the Black community and engage in authentic dialogue with them about it; and 2) Black students want to see themselves in the curriculum in meaningful ways, and they want to learn more about their own histories. As English teachers, how do we begin to make this shift in our classroom environment and curriculum? The following are a few suggestions from seminal texts in our field that have become mentor texts for me.

Confront Your Biases: Racial Literacy

Dr. Yolanda Sealey-Ruiz (2021) provides us with a framework to help English teachers become the educators that our Black students need us to be. The first step is to begin with racial literacy:

> Racial literacy is a skill and practice by which individuals can probe the existence of racism and examine the effects of race and institutionalized systems on their experiences and representation in US society. Students who have this skill can discuss the implications of race and American racism in constructive ways. A desired outcome of racial literacy in an outwardly racist society like America is for members of the dominant racial category to adopt an antiracist stance and persons of color to resist a victim stance. Thus, racial literacy in English classrooms is the ability to read, discuss, and write about situations that involve race and racism. (p. 2)

The process of espousing and teaching racial literacy is twofold. First, white teachers must "adopt an antiracist stance," which means that they must spend time confronting and reflecting on their biases and understand how their biases show up in their curriculum and in the ways in which they engage with their students. Sealey-Ruiz (2022) has developed a healing process called the "Archaeology of the Self" that supports teachers in confronting their racial bias and helping them learn how to move from a place of critical reflection to a place of critical love.

When educators have done the work on themselves, they can then effectively teach students how to "read, discuss, and write about situations that involve race and racism" (Sealey-Ruiz, 2022). Second, while teachers must acknowledge the injustices that Black students face in meaningful ways, the goal is to empower them, not victimize them. This means that teachers must foster classroom environments in which students learn about civic engagement, advocacy, and think about ways to bring change to their communities.

Get to Know Your Students: Humanizing Pedagogy

As English teachers, we want to create curriculum that is affirming, empowering, and humanizing; however, we cannot provide our students with what they need if we do not know them. Shamari Reid's (2024) *Humans Who Teach: A Guide for Centering Love, Justice, and Liberation in Schools* provides teachers with practical ways to create classroom culture that is rooted in love and that encourages students to share the most vulnerable parts of themselves. Reid challenges teachers to reflect on key essential questions such as: "As a human who teaches, in what ways does my approach to teaching respond to actual (and not assumed) circumstances and challenges my students are navigating?" (p. 66). Reid shares his own personal experiences in the secondary classroom, where reflective journaling was a core practice that allowed Reid's students to learn about his life and vice versa. Through this practice, Reid was able to collaborate with his students to support some of the educational needs of new migrants and their families.

Refining Your Practice: Culturally and Historically Responsive Teaching and Learning

I am a teacher educator in an urban English education teacher preparation program. At the beginning of every semester, I ask my preservice and early career teachers to reflect on the legacy they want to leave as educators—through their interpersonal relationships with students and through their curriculum. Gholdy Muhammad's (2023) *Unearthing Joy: A Guide to Culturally and Historically Responsive Teaching and Learning* has helped me in facilitating this work with my students. Muhammad explains, "Curriculum defined as legacy and legacy building means that what we teach and how we teach it must leave an imprint on the lives of our students. It should feel special and enduring. Such curriculum should encourage and enable students to feel, and act toward improving the self and the world" (p. 123). If we as teachers desire to be "civic agents" (Mirra & Morrell, 2011) who empower our students to become civically engaged, we have to identify the areas in our curriculum that may hinder that goal. Muhammad provides us with some critical questions to ask ourselves when looking at our curriculum such as: "Does my current curriculum implicitly or explicitly contribute to others' hurt, harm or pain?" (p. 124).

Looking toward the Future

As the opening anecdote about former President Donald Trump reveals, our democracy is at risk. The future of this country will be in the hands of our students, and it is our responsibility to cultivate their hearts and minds. Moreover, we must support them in becoming democratic citizens who make the needs of *all* people a priority in the United States. The secondary English classroom has the potential to be a place in which this type of learning and unlearning can be nurtured.

Works Cited

Anderson, R. E., Saleem, F. T., & Huguley, J. P. (2019). Choosing to see the racial stress that afflicts our Black students. *Phi Delta Kappan, 101*(3), 20–25.

Barnum, M., & Belsha, K. (2020, June 2). *Protests, donations, lesson plans: How the education world is responding to George Floyd's killing.* Chalkbeat. www.chalkbeat.org/2020/6/2/21278591/education-schools-george-floyd-racism/

Cohen, C., Kahne, J., & Marshall, J. With Anderson, V., Brower, M., and Knight, D. (2018). *Let's go there: Race, ethnicity and a Lived Civics approach to civic education.* GenForward.

Crenshaw, K. (1989). Demarginalizing the intersection of race and sex: A Black feminist critique of antidiscrimination doctrine, feminist theory and antiracist politics. *University of Chicago Legal Forum, 1989*(1), 139–167.

Freire, P. (1970). *Pedagogy of the oppressed.* Continuum.

Ladson-Billings, G. (2013). "Stakes is high": Educating new century students. *Journal of Negro Education, 82*(2), 105–110.

Legal Defense Fund. *Criminal justice and policing: Qualified immunity FAQ.* (n.d.). Legal Defense Fund. www.naacpldf.org/qualified-immunity/

Levinson, M. (2010). The civic empowerment gap: Defining the problem and locating solutions. In L. Sherrod, J. Torney-Purta, & C. Flanagan (Eds.), *Handbook of research on civic engagement* (pp. 331–361). John Wiley & Sons.

Love, B. (2019). *We want to do more than survive: Abolitionist teaching and the pursuit of educational freedom.* Beacon Press.

Mirra, M., & Garcia, A. (2023). *Civics for the world to come: Committing to democracy in every classroom.* W. W. Norton & Company.

Mirra, M., & Morrell, E. (2011). Teachers as civic agents: Toward a critical democratic theory of urban teacher development. *Journal of Teacher Education, 62*(4), 408–420.

Muhammad, G. (2020). *Cultivating genius: An equity framework for culturally and historically responsive literacy.* Scholastic.

Muhammad, G. (2023). *Unearthing joy: A guide to culturally and historically responsive teaching and learning.* Scholastic.

Muhammad, G. E., & Haddix M. (2016). Centering Black girls' literacies: A review of literature on the multiple ways of knowing of Black girls. *English Education, 48*(4), 299–336.

Price-Dennis, D. (2016). Developing curriculum to support Black girls' literacies in digital spaces. *English Education, 48*(4), 337–361.

Reid, S. (2024). *Humans who teach: A guide for centering love, justice, and liberation in schools.* Heinemann.

Sealey-Ruiz, Y. (2016). Why Black girls' literacies matter: New literacies for a new era. *English Education, 48*(4), 290–297.

Sealey-Ruiz, Y. (2021). *Racial literacy.* National Council of Teachers of English. https://ncte.org/wp-content/uploads/2021/04/SquireOfficePolicyBrief_RacialLiteracy_April2021.pdf

Sealey-Ruiz, Y. (2022). An Archaeology of Self for our times: Another talk to teachers. *English Journal, 111*(5), 21–26.

Trump, D. (2024, May 1). *Donald Trump holds rally in Wisconsin on 5/01/24* [Speech transcript]. Rev. www.rev.com/blog/transcripts/donald-trump-holds-rally-in-wisconsin-on-5-01-24

Promoting Criticality through Research and Texts on Black Youth Educational Activism

GLENDA D. CHISHOLM

Lessons from a Black Youth Activist

The Civil Rights era provided many lessons about fighting for equality. Activists protested in many ways, including marches, speeches, rallies, and litigations in court. Most relevant to this study are protests in the form of direct action. Direct action was a hands-on, overt attempt to influence change and is Black youth activists' legacy when fighting for social change (Bynum, 2013). Widely noted examples of direct-action campaigns include Black high school and college students who protested in the 1960s in the form of sit-ins, walkouts, and making demands. In this study, I work alongside six Black youths in middle and high school, studying the educational experiences of Black youths and the ways those Black youths promote change. I ask, *How do students perceive and respond to literacy curriculum that promotes criticality where Black youth histories and cultural practices are at the center?*

Black Student Demands and Demand Pedagogy

A Google search of the phrase "Black student demands" brings up over 1.5 billion historical and contemporary results in just over two seconds. The results on demands are notable because writing lists of demands requires both a heightened consciousness and competence in reading and writing skills. Critiques within demands have included an examination of textbooks, inclusion of Black history courses in schools, drug treatment for community members, administrative transparency, equity in funds disbursement, etc. Historical examples have been documented and contemporary examples can be found on Black student union websites. The following is the concluding statement written by New York high school youth in 1969:

> We are sure that you, the Black Community, will recognize the long overdue changes that [our] demands call for. We grew tired of waiting for you adults to really wake up and understand what we have been trying to tell you all these years. Those "so-called" schools you were rushing us off to every morning represented to us cruel prisons where we were sentenced to serve our time without a hope of parole. (Winn, 2021, p. 534)

Youths' comparison of schools to "cruel prisons" was ahead of scholarship on schools as institutions of social reproduction and has remained consistent to work of scholars such as Alexander (2010). Studying demands offer one way to foster youth's criticality or their skills in understanding, naming, interrogating, and disrupting oppression.

To write demands, students identified issues of importance, studied texts related to their concern, and conducted individual photovoice projects on their schooling experiences. I facilitated lessons in which youths and I engaged with multimodal texts on Black youth's educational experiences. I also introduced them to activist literacies or ways of reading, writing, and speaking to critique and dismantle oppression (Crisco, 2009). I framed each lesson using Muhammad's (2020) Histories, Identities, Languages, and Liberation (HILL) framework. In this chapter, I show analysis of how texts on Black youth educational experiences can be used as a culturally and historically responsive approach to literacy learning.

Literature Review and Conceptual Framework

In this section, I discuss frameworks used to engage with students on this project. In addition to reading, writing, and analyzing texts, youths documented their schools' strengths and challenges using photos and written analysis. The group employed youth participatory action research (YPAR) (Cammarota & Fine, 2008), Black participatory action research (BPAR) (Drame & Irby, 2016), and the HILL framework (Muhammad, 2020). Each method or framework promotes equity and contributes to participants' expansion of criticality. I review literature from each of these approaches to research and learning.

YPAR, BPAR, and HILL

Youth participatory action research is a method of critical inquiry in which youth and adult participants work collaboratively to understand and act in order to change oppressive conditions impacting their communities (Cammarota & Fine, 2008; Morrell, 2012). Each person participating in the process is a researcher bringing knowledge from their lived experiences or academic studies. Positioning youth as experts or co-researchers in YPAR differs from traditional applications of pedagogy in classroom spaces where students are merely recipients of knowledge (Burke & Hadley, 2018). Participatory action research projects provide a frame for thinking through a common issue and then developing solutions for social justice in a community.

To facilitate students' thinking around community challenges and solutions, we employed Morrell's (2008) Critical Cycle of Praxis (CCP) (see Figure 1) using the CCP facilitated discussion of texts we read as a group and photos students created during our research. We also used the CCP to evaluate our research progress during the inquiry process. Since I conducted this study alongside Black youths, I conceptualized a methodological framework of YPAR and BPAR called Black participatory research with youth. Drame and Irby (2016) described BPAR as action research projects done by members of the Black community for the improvement of a shared issue in the Black community. By centering race, BPAR empowers Black communities to create change independently. As a result, I also curated curriculum resources centering Black youth voices. Last, I used Muhammad's (2020) HILL equity framework for lesson planning. I began with state language arts and social studies standards and added criticality and identity. The HILL framework provided a practical application for cultivating learners' identity, skills, intellect, and criticality. I explicitly cultivated students' identities, skills, and intellect through reading, writing, and discussing the experiences of Black youth in schools and their own experiences. To cultivate their criticality, the group read and discussed texts to understand contextual factors influencing other Black youth to fight for youth social change and texts that detail Black youth-created change. Then, participating youths planned ways to facilitate change in their schools.

Adolescent Literacies

Another area of scholarship from which I drew was adolescent literacies and literacy practices in Black families and communities. Black youth engage in literacy practices in their homes and communities that may differ from the literacy practices they are asked to show proficiency in at school (Kinloch, Burkhard, & Penn, 2017). This means that educators are missing opportunities to connect learning to their students in meaningful ways. Educators wanting to teach students differently would benefit from seeking methods of teaching that bring in students' home experiences; instruction should not be singular or monolithic (Heath, 1983; Tatum, 2013). In this study, I drew upon students' fluency in visual and technological literacies after noticing that youth-exemplified media knowledge was not being drawn upon in their traditional schooling experience. As a result, we used phones throughout our study to scan barcodes, create images, and communicate as a group.

Relying on phones in our study differed from the practices youth experienced in their traditional schooling practices, where they were asked to put phones away to learn. No-phone policies in schools might prevent educators from helping students make meaningful connections. These policies are detached from students'

Figure 1. Critical Cycle of Praxis (CCP) (adapted from Morrell, 2008)

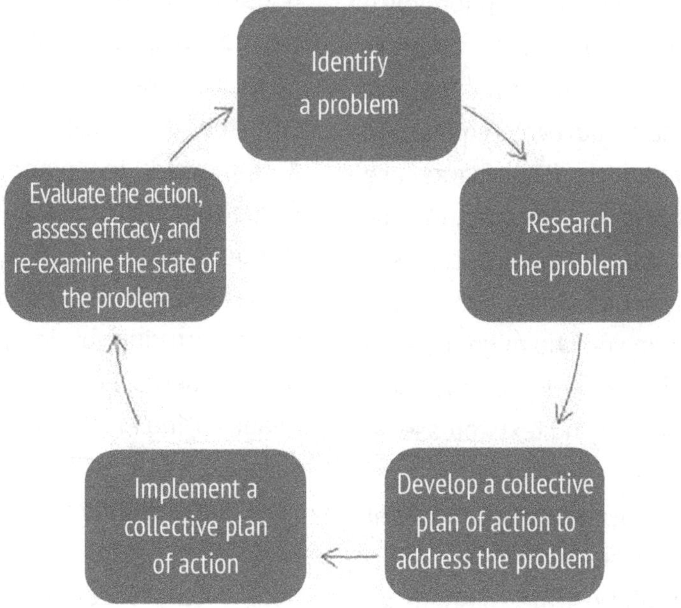

cultural practices and serve to separate school from their daily lives. Further, such policies interfere with students' ability to be fully engaged in their learning experiences, mirroring larger systemic issues of control over minoritized communities. This means that teachers should teach in ways that are relevant and responsive to youths' lived experiences (Ladson-Billings, 1994; Paris, 2012). Ultimately, I sought to use relevant methods and resources to create learning opportunities that pushed the boundaries of traditional schooling to promote liberation.

Methodology

Over six months, six youths and I met face-to-face and virtually to learn, build community, and discuss the youths' research as a collective taking part in a PAR project. The students' research goal was to create a project that honored what they loved about and what they wanted to change about their schools using a participatory action research method called photovoice (Wang & Burris, 1997). During photovoice, participants document strengths and challenges of their community by creating photographic images and writing narratives. The goal of a photovoice project is to understand a community from the perspective of a community member, to highlight an issue of inequity, and to advocate equity and justice to their communities. Participants use photos and narratives as a tool to communicate. The idea is that visuals and language create a more complete idea than one alone and provide a clear idea to those in power who might be able to influence community change. For an overview of the lessons and accompanying texts, please go to https://bit.ly/NCTECivics.

The six students, or co-researchers, brought an insider perspective, and my role as a researcher in academia allowed me to share an outside perspective. We complemented one another. For example, I might have perspectives that youth may not have considered because they are deeply embedded in the cultural phenomenon of schooling they seek to challenge and vice versa. While students conducted their research, I also conducted research in which I sought to answer two questions: *1) What perceptions do Black students have about a literacy curriculum that promotes criticality where Black youth histories are at the center?* and *2) How do Black youth respond to literacy curriculum that promotes criticality where Black youth histories are at the center?* In this project, I worked as a facilitator and a researcher. My methods for both were deeply intertwined and related. I briefly describe both below.

Teacher and Researcher Methods

I used Muhammad's (2020) HILL framework to bolster state standards by attending to students' identity and criticality in addition to skills and intellect, which are the basis of state standards. Muhammad (2020) defines literacy as skills and proficiencies tied to identity, intellectualism, liberation, and power. Using this definition, she outlines the four components of her Histories, Identities, Languages, and Liberation (HILL) framework to include identities, skills, intellectualism, and criticality or critical consciousness that provide a framework for planning lessons. The HILL framework is situated in culturally relevant and responsive theories. In this work, teachers act as guides to building student knowledge and skills while nurturing joy, identity, and criticality with their students. For an outline on how I created images using Muhammad's framework, please go to https://bit.ly/NCTECivics.

I collected data to include semi-structured interviews, student work artifacts, images, field notes, reflections, and jottings (Charmaz, 2006; DeWalt & DeWalt, 2011; Roulston, 2010).

Secondary data included text messages, email messages, and recordings of group discussions during photo group sessions.

Students Building Knowledge: Process and Findings

During this study, I worked alongside students as a teacher-researcher cultivating their critical literacy skills as they wrote and thought together. Experiences to cultivate critical literacies included visiting schools (public, charter, and private), photography lessons, creating images, and reading, discussing, and analyzing texts. Youths researched their personal experiences by documenting strengths and areas for growth in their schools. At the end of the project, youth participants collectively wrote a list of statements detailing what they deserve as Black youths in schools today entitled "We Deserve."

Building Knowledge through Text Analysis

I had several learning goals for students. Primarily, I wanted them to gain greater knowledge about their own and other Black people's experiences in education. I also strived to foster greater sociopolitical and historical knowledge to understand the context in which people's experiences occurred, ways to advocate for change, and community empowerment through research. To gain knowledge in these areas, students participated in gallery walks, analyzed texts, participated in discussions, visited five schools, and learned from a professional photographer, created images, and analyzed images.

We began our research with two gallery walks. One gallery walk focused on Black educational history and photography; the other focused on photovoice and ethics. We also studied multimodal texts. Students analyzed texts throughout the project, and we often referred to previous texts to make connections to the images students created. For a list of the multimodal text sets, please go to https://bit.ly/NCTECivics.

I began with the gallery walks to encourage collaboration, critical thinking, and conversation. The students worked in groups, moving through different stations where I posted QR codes with chart paper on which they could interact with multimodal forms of text and share knowledge with one another. During the first gallery walk, I provided eight images and short narratives. The images in Figure 2 show students working in a group to respond to the text and reading what other groups have posted.

Figure 2. Gallery walk

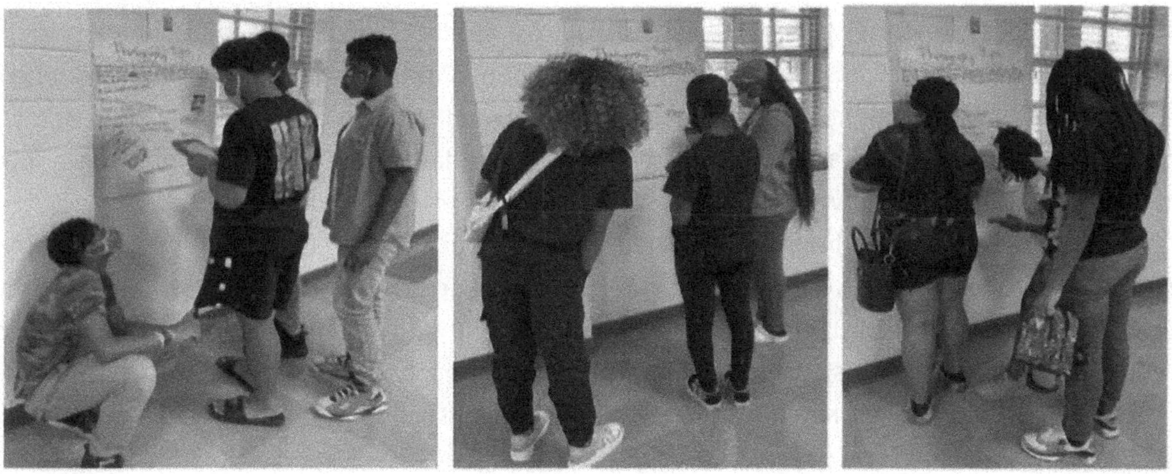

Each image and narrative highlighted education from a Black historical perspective. I began with evidence of education in Africa by creating a timeline predating slavery and ending in the 1960s. This was vital because oftentimes schools reproduce dominant narratives of Black life beginning at slavery without mentioning the intellect and creativity of Africans before colonization (King, 2017). After reading the images and text, the students sat in a group and discussed the images. The second gallery walk also consisted of images and written text. In the second gallery walk, I shifted the focus from Black education to photography. The second gallery walk focused on ways to photograph images creatively, Black photographers, taking ethical photos, and students who had experiences with a photovoice project. This gallery walk provided youths with examples of Black photography practices to demonstrate a research tool of resistance using representations of Blackness that are creative and that we deem are necessary.

Building Knowledge through School Visits and Image Creation

After building contextual knowledge through activities such as the gallery walks, students discussed their personal experiences in school. Together, the group began with a brainstorming session to discuss what they loved and wanted to change about their schools. The youths also brainstormed how they might create images to represent their ideas. They came up with a list of ideas; for example, they loved Black teachers, classes that look nice, and the feeling of their school being like mini Historically Black Colleges and Universities (HBCUs). For things they would like to change they discussed the lack of resources and food and promoted the need to have therapy.

Students and I took learning journeys to five schools (public, charter, and private) within a five-mile radius of where the summer enrichment program took place. During the visits, students toured and posed questions about the school to principals, teachers, and students who attended that school. The school visits took place in the summer so in some cases, the student we talked to was a member of our group who had attended the school during the fall and spring. Only one student who took pictures at her school during summer school visits used her pictures for her final photovoice project. The remainder of the group returned to their home schools to create images in the fall. When students created images, they brought them to our weekly meetings and completed a SHOWED method. The SHOWED method is a tool for analyzing photos during photovoice projects in which students respond to five questions: 1) What do you **S**ee here? 2) What is really **H**appening here? 3) How does this relate to **O**ur lives? 4) **W**hy does this condition **E**xist? 5) What can we **D**o about it? Each letter from SHOWED helps students to think through the importance of this picture within their project. Using the chart, youths responded to prompts to organize the thoughts they could use in their photo narratives. After using the SHOWED chart to analyze their photos, students explained their images to the group, and then the group offered comments and feedback. From image creation to analysis, youths developed their identities, skills, intellectualism, and criticality.

Figure 3 *(see next page)* is an example of an image created by Marley, an eighth-grade student who is demonstrating criticality. She discussed how students had not benefitted from the school garden because no one used it.

Figure 3. Marley's SHOWED method and garden image

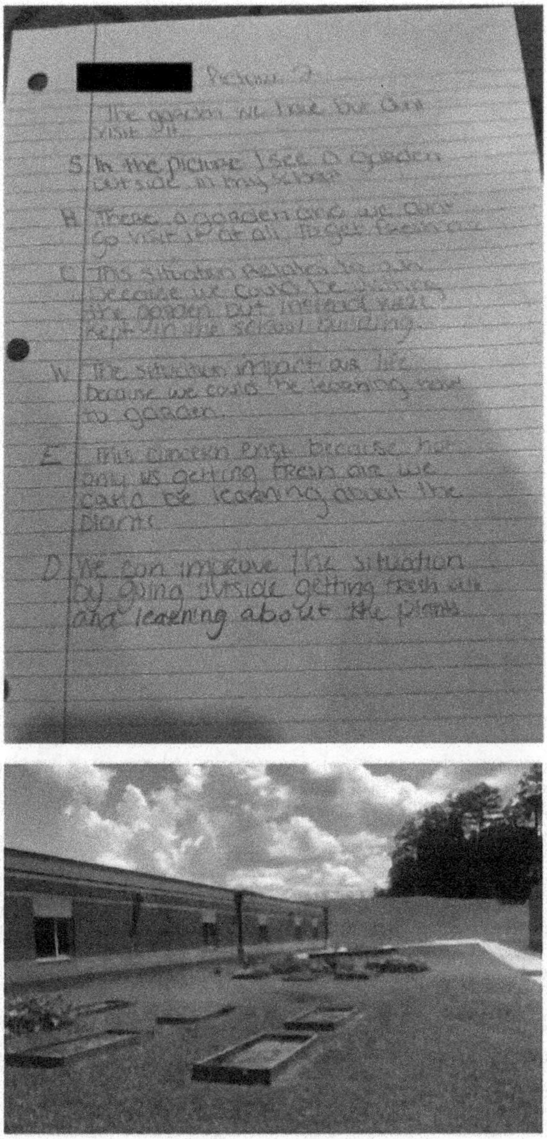

Building Knowledge during Image Creation and Analysis

Since writing is essential to a photovoice project, I was able to integrate writing instruction naturally. However, student interview data revealed that the SHOWED method was also helpful for students when writing and reading. Using the SHOWED method fostered critical thinking and skillful communication that helped develop participants' written and communication skills. Students had consistent practice because they created a minimum of ten images and analyzed them. Below, Yara, a tenth-grade participant, discussed the project and how it helped her to improve in writing and reading.

> I would describe photovoice as an informational learning project. Okay, like a project where you can also have fun with but you're learning, you're gaining something from it . . . your writing skills, your reading skills, your information. Everything that you learn, you're gaining something from this project, not just the, you know, go to school, take a picture, or write an essay about something. It's, like, how you feel. Or when we read a book, you're really gaining something. You're learning new things that a regular school and classes will not teach you. (Final program interview, December 2021)

As noted by Yara, this process can be one that strengthens students' skills while also being a joyful experience. The name of the method, photovoice, suggests images are more powerful when they are accompanied by words, and the SHOWED photo analysis facilitated depth of examination. In the project, students also regularly read and discussed texts about Black youth creating social change as an exercise to cultivate criticality as the students were analyzing their images. According to student-combined experiences, reading text and photo analysis deepened their intellectual knowledge in history and literacy skills.

Seven themes emerged from my analysis. I found three themes when analyzing youths' perceptions of literacy. Youth perceptions of literacy included knowledge expansion,

Figure 4. Julian's presentation slide, narrative and deserve statement

self-expression, and enjoyable moments. In response to the youths' responses to the program, I found four themes when analyzing: youth gained confidence in their literacy skills, demonstrated agency and leadership, emphasized the need for Blackness, and responded critically. Julian's slide above illustrates the need for Blackness and responding critically.

Like Julian, all students wrote "We Deserve" statements to accompany their images, detailing what Black youth in schools today deserve. Participants discussed not needing to make demands. And when I asked why they preferred to say *deserve* instead of *demand*, Quinn, a twelfth-grade student, noted, "The Black community do deserve a lot more without having to say demand" (Final program interview, 2021).

Implications for Teachers

Drawing from the rich history of Black youth activists, this study intertwined literacy and activism using a participatory research methodology. This work has four suggestions for teachers to consider in their practice when cultivating students' criticality. First, begin with students' stories and histories. Black history does not begin with slavery, not in Europe or the United States; it begins in Africa. Next, co-construct projects with youth. Students informed many of the researcher moves in this project. It was because of their input that we visited schools in the summer of 2021. Further, build autonomy in literacy projects. As noted in Yara's quote earlier, building upon students' knowledge and lived experiences honors their agency in the learning process. Finally, provide students with opportunities to study and research their communities. Julian researched his community, which resulted in him wanting to learn more Black history.

Teachers wishing to engage in a similar project with their students might reflect upon the following questions:

1. How might I teach in ways that return students to their cultural legacies?

2. What ways are youth impacted daily that might encourage them to use their pens and literacies to spark activism for social change?
3. In what ways can I make my learning space one that actively promotes liberation?

This study created space for adolescents to cultivate their criticality. We actively worked against educational systems that have historically oppressed Black and other people of color to promote liberation. Our work provides educators and policymakers an opportunity to shape learning environments in ways that the students find relatable. It also shapes students' political identities and contributes to their literacy development in ways that are responsive culturally and historically.

Works Cited

Alexander, M. (2010). *The new Jim Crow: Mass incarceration in the age of colorblindness.* The New Press.

Biondi, M. (2012). *The Black revolution on campus.* University of California Press.

Bundy, T. (2017). "Revolutions happen through young people!" The Black student movement in the Boston Public Schools, 1968–1971. *Journal of Urban History, 43*(2), 273–293. https://doi.org/10.1177/0096144216688277

Burke, K. J., & Hadley, H. L. (2018). I'm empowered by a better connection. *The High School Journal, 101*(4), 217-235.

Bynum, T. (2013). *NAACP youth and the fight for Black Freedom, 1936–1965.* Univ. of Tennessee Press.

Cammarota, J., & Fine, M. (2008). Youth participatory action research: A pedagogy for transformational resistance. In J. Cammarota & M. Fine (Eds.), *Revolutionizing education: Youth participatory action research in motion* (pp. 1–12). Routledge.

Charmaz, K. (2006). *Constructing grounded theory: A practical guide through qualitative analysis.* SAGE.

Crisco, V. (2009). Activating activist literacy: Discovering dispositions for civic identity development. *Composition Studies, 37*(2), 31–51.

DeWalt, K. M., & DeWalt, B. R. (2011). *Participant observation: A guide for fieldworkers.* Rowman & Littlefield.

Drame, E. R., & Irby, D. J. (Eds.). (2016). *Black participatory research: Power, identity, and the struggle for justice in education.* Palgrave Macmillan.

Franklin, V. P. (2021). *The young crusaders: The untold story of the children and teenagers who galvanized the Civil Rights Movement.* Beacon Press.

Heath, S. B. (1983). *Ways with words: Language, life, and work in communities and classrooms.* Cambridge University Press.

Jocson, K. M. (2006). "The best of both worlds": Youth poetry as social critique and form of empowerment. In S. Ginwright, P. Noguera, & J. Cammarota (Eds.), *Beyond resistance! Youth activism and community change: New democratic possibilities for practice and policy for America's yout*h (pp. 129–147). Routledge.

King, L. J. (2017). The status of Black history in U.S. schools and society. *Social Education, 81*(1), 14–18.

Kinloch, V., Burkhard, T., & Penn, C. (2017). When school is not enough: Understanding the lives and literacies of Black youth. *Research in the Teaching of English, 52*(1), 34-54.

Ladson-Billings, G. (1994). *The Dreamkeepers: Successful teachers of African-American children.* Jossey-Bass.

Morrell, E. (2012). 21st-century literacies, critical media pedagogies, and language arts. *The Reading Teacher, 66*(4), 300-302.

Muhammad, G. E. (2019). Protest, power, and possibilities: The need for agitation literacies. *Journal of Adolescent & Adult Literacy, 63*(3), 351–355.

Muhammad, G. E. (2020). *Cultivating genius: An equity framework for culturally and historically responsive literacy.* Scholastic.

Paris, D. (2012). Culturally sustaining pedagogy: A needed change in stance, terminology, and practice. *Educational Researcher, 41*(3), 93–97. https://doi.org/10.3102/0013189X12441244

Roulston, K. (2010). *Reflective interviewing: A guide to theory & practice.* SAGE.

Stovall, D. (2006). From hunger strike to high school: Youth development, social justice, and school formation. In S. Ginwright, P. Noguera, & J. Cammarota (Eds.), *Beyond resistance! Youth activism and community change: New democratic possibilities for practice and policy for America's youth* (pp. 97–110). Routledge.

Tatum, A. W. (2013). Toward a more anatomically complete model of literacy instruction: A focus on African American male adolescents and texts. In D. E. Alvermann, N. J. Unrau, & R. B. Ruddell (Eds.), *Theoretical models and processes of reading* (6th ed., pp. 611–634). International Reading Association.

Wang, C. C., & Burris, M. A. (1997). Photovoice: Concept, methodology, and use for participatory needs assessment. *Health Education & Behavior, 24*(3), 369–387.

Winn, M. T. (2021). Futures matter: Creating just futures in this age of hyper-incarceration. *Peabody Journal of Education, 96*(5), 527–539.

Practicing Black Linguistic Justice at an HBCU in the Age of the Stop W.O.K.E. Act

HYO KYUNG WOO

Governor Ron DeSantis of Florida has been outspoken about his disapproval of what he refers to as woke ideologies, especially in Florida's educational system, since 2021. His administration has advocated for changes to school curricula, aiming to promote what he calls "objective" education and to push back against what he sees as overly politicized or biased teaching (Florida Department of Education, 2021). This includes attempts to restructure Florida schools' teaching of history, civics, and social studies to emphasize "traditional American values" rather than "divisive" or controversial topics like critical race theory (CRT), a theory that examines how racism is ingrained in institutions and laws. DeSantis has been a vocal opponent of CRT and signed an executive order banning CRT from being taught in Florida's public schools, arguing that it promotes division rather than unity (DeSantis, 2021).

Many Florida educators are concerned that outlawing CRT in the classroom will limit conversations about racism and its continuing effects, therefore impeding attempts to solve systemic inequalities that underprivileged people must endure (Allen, 2024). DeSantis's policy has also raised concern among my colleagues at Edward Waters University. It is frightening to hear about how it has affected other institutions in our area, such as when the English department at the University of Central Florida had to remove their statement regarding racial justice or when a professor was prohibited from teaching about sexuality and race in her sociology class (Osorio, 2022). As faculty members at an institution heavily dependent on government funding for underprivileged minority students, we find ourselves self-censoring and questioning our teaching by constantly wondering what would be "appropriate" to teach in class in the age of the Stop W.O.K.E. Act.

Amid confusion and worries about the new regulations in Florida, our campus became a target of a racially motivated shooting on August 26, 2023. Targeting Black people, a 21-year-old white man arrived on our campus carrying both a rifle and a handgun. He left manifestos that included his hatred of Black people and a detailed shooting strategy, stating he "wants to kill [the N-words]" (Stepzinski, 2023). When our students flagged down and told campus security guard Antonio Bailey, the gunman was stopped and chased off from our faculty parking lot outside the university library. The shooter then went to a nearby Dollar General and began shooting at random Black customers, killing three people in all.

The EWU president, Dr. A. Zachary Faison Jr., suspected that the gunman had first intended to target EWU, the first HBCU in Florida, because of its historic and symbolic role in the New Town community, the heart of the Black community in Jacksonville. The fatal incident deeply frightened our students and the campus community, resulting in a long-lasting collective trauma. This led us to realize that our beloved campus, where we study, eat, and hang out, was no longer a safe place, and my students became the subjects of hate and violence because of their skin color.

Overall, the ongoing effect of Florida's Stop W.O.K.E. Act and the racially motivated shooting both internally and externally provoked our faculty and students to delve into what it means to engage in civic education at HBCUs. It also challenged my pedagogical role as an English instructor at an HBCU by causing me to ask myself how I can support my students and colleagues during this challenging time. As a teacher of language and literature, I made the decision to actively incorporate the theme of Black Linguistic Justice into my first-year composition class.

Civic Education and Black Linguistic Justice at HBCUs

Throughout history, HBCUs have had a significant impact on developing the range of knowledge, skills, and dispositions necessary for effective citizenship in a democratic society. The origins of civic education at HBCUs can be attributed to their foundational principles and historical mission. HBCUs, which were founded after the Civil War, served as symbols of hope for recently freed Black Americans. These institutions were established based on the belief that education is the crucial factor in achieving liberation and empowerment. HBCUs not only focused on academic instruction but also placed a high priority on fostering moral character, civic virtue, and social responsibility in their students. Early leaders of HBCUs such as Howard University, Fisk University, and the Tuskegee Institute (now Tuskegee University) integrated civic education into their curriculum to negotiate the intricate challenges of post-emancipation society. The objective of these courses was to cultivate in students a strong sense of civic responsibility, effective leadership skills, and a steadfast dedication to promoting social justice—an ideology that continues to be at the core of the purpose of HBCUs in the present day.

Aligned with this mission, first-year composition courses play a fundamental role in the liberal arts curriculum at HBCUs, providing students with essential writing, critical thinking, and effective communication skills. HBCUs can enrich the educational experience and empower students to be informed, engaged citizens by incorporating civic education into composition classes (Cokley, 2002). This integration can manifest in different forms, such as including civic themes that are pertinent to Black American communities in writing assignments. Within this framework, I designed a course that required students to analyze and assess the linguistic formations and hierarchies of higher educational institutions in the US. It asked students to recognize bias and discrimination in the educational system and to engage in responsible citizenship under the concept of Black Linguistic Justice.

Black scholars, such as April Baker-Bell, bell hooks, Carmen Kynard, and others, have highlighted the discriminatory character of English education toward Black students in higher institutions in the United States. The Black Linguistic Justice movement seeks to promote the acknowledgement and legitimacy of Black language variants while contesting linguistic injustice and advocating for linguistic diversity (Baker-Bell & Kynard, 2024). At its core, it seeks to tackle the inherent prejudices and inequalities that diminish Black languages and dialects in educational, social, and cultural settings. The movement highlights the significance of acknowledging and valuing linguistic variety, specifically within the Black community.

Since Black Linguistic Justice pedagogy advocates confronting linguistic discrimination, it provides my students with an opportunity to reconsider the devaluation or stigmatization of Black languages. This process motivates them to question various forms of discrimination, such as negative stereotypes, biased language assessments, and discriminatory hiring practices based on linguistic background. This becomes particularly important to my students, who have continuously struggled in their first-year composition classes and have received unfavorable feedback from their previous English teachers, who simply disregarded their writings as "inappropriate" or "ignorant." Consequently, I have observed that my students often exhibit reluctance in sharing their written work with me and feel embarrassed when they make spelling mistakes during class:

> I've been told that how I speak is wrong and is not how a proper person would speak. Being in the Black community, we are told to be proud of where we come from and hold our head high no matter the circumstances, but then we go into the real world, and we are judged simply by how we speak. In high school, I have written many good essays but because my teacher didn't like that I spoke with my true authenticity she would deduct points from my assignment. (Jada Burroughs)

By equipping my students with critical views on the politics of language and racism, I aimed to enable them to effectively negotiate the intricate dynamics of racial violence and to actively engage in public discourse that supports civic causes and social justice initiatives. In doing so, my students can cultivate a more profound comprehension of their responsibilities as proactive members of society and evolve into civically involved citizens who champion positive changes in their communities.

Although the incorporation of civic education and Black Linguistic Justice into a composition course provides many advantages, it also poses difficulties and challenges. One obstacle is to acknowledge that Black language is not a homogenous entity, and not all Black students at HBCUs employ American Englishes. Edward Waters University has a student population of approximately 1,200, made up of 85 percent Black students, 6 percent white students, 4 percent Hispanic students, and 5 percent multiethnic students. While the Black student population is predominantly represented, it is crucial to be aware that many Black students come from diverse international backgrounds, resulting in the use of several Black languages. Hence, exploring Black Linguistic Justice inside and outside of the United States can prove highly advantageous for our students, given the expanding variety of the student population at HBCUs in the present era (Brown & Dancy, 2017). The presence of global Black diaspora groups, including African, African American, Afro-Brazilian, Caribbean, and Colombian students, contributes to the ethnic diversity of HBCUs by adding complexity to the concept of racial heterogeneity within the experiences of Black students. For example, certain international students in my class expressed the previously unnoticed difference in the use of Black languages between themselves and American students at HBCUs:

> As a person of African descent, I can clearly recall my own experiences of navigating the different uses of Black language when I first came to the States, in and out of the classroom. Growing up in West Africa, I used different Black language when I attended school in the US. (Caleb Borketey)

Furthermore, the rising enrollment of non-Black minorities at HBCUs aligns with the fundamental objective of promoting Black Linguistic Justice, as it reflects the growing diversity and language within these institutions. The Black Linguistic Justice pedagogy might suggest a resolution to ethically acknowledge each other's linguistic and cultural differences in our extremely globalized society beyond HBCUs.

Teaching Narrative: Black Linguistic Justice within an HBCU Classroom

In the fall 2023 semester, I taught English Composition 1102, an upper-level first-year composition course, at Edward Waters University. Based on a class survey, the racial composition of the students in this course closely resembled that of the student population at EWU. The demographic composition included 89 percent Black American, 6 percent white, and 5 percent Hispanic individuals, with a male-female ratio of 42 percent to 58 percent. The majority of students indicated they were unfamiliar with the concept of Black Linguistic Justice and had not contemplated the discrepancy between their vernacular language and academic language. Nevertheless, they frequently recounted instances of facing discrimination, humiliation, and condemnation due to their use of Black language in educational and professional settings:

> My earliest memory of writing in Black language was in third grade. My reading teacher would give us essays, and we would have to write them based on the prompt provided. In the beginning, I wrote the essays exactly as I spoke in Black English, and I would get points knocked off because it wasn't in standard English. Meanwhile, me and my friends would meet up at a light pole every day after school and discuss what was going on in our day-to-day lives. Words like "you lyin" "stop Flaggin" and "Rate him" were most commonly used in our conversations. I remember growing up, and my grandma would tell me I need to stop speaking in that "Ghetto" language and speak proper English. To her, if you spoke proper standard English, you would get better opportunities and even farther in life. (Chinaya Isnadin)

The majority of my students' essays detailed their encounters with discrimination due to their use of Black language. Significantly, their experiences frequently entailed a story about school, where they experienced persistent rejection and failure:

> As a Black student with a disability, I understand the challenges and frustration that Black students face from the beginning in academia, which often left me feeling inadequate and different. For instance, during my English classes in high school, I often heard my white peers scoffed and

> scorned me for not only my disability but my speech patterns. It was things like how I would say "e'en on my best day, ion know who might support me." When I read my paper in front of classes, I had to meet with embarrassment and ridicule from peers because of my speech impediment along with how I would say "e'en, ion, ain't, frfr, ikyl, etc." I was called "uneducated" because I lacked "sophistication." Not only did this leave me unmotivated, but this also left me in a feeling of rejection, making me think how the educational system failed Black students so easy and fast. (Winston Cassan)

Upon reviewing the student essays, I gained insight into the reasons behind my students' difficulties in trusting teachers and these students' self-defeating mindsets. After observing racialized linguistic bias against my students, I assigned them a reading entitled "This Ain't Another Statement! This is a DEMAND for Black Linguistic Justice!" In July 2020, a group of experts and educators specializing in Black language and literacy issued a stimulating statement, arguing for Black Linguistic Justice in conjunction with the #BlackLivesMatter movement (Baker-Bell, 2020).

My students' response essays demonstrated a diverse array of viewpoints about this controversial issue. Many students astutely point out the existence of a structural double standard when it comes to the use of Black language in what they call the "real world" compared to their everyday community. Their voices also expressed concern for fully adapting Black Linguistic Justice to school curriculum, because of their realistic issues such as hiring opportunities and academic assignments:

> The argument about how Black Linguistic Justice in college English education can benefit Black students in academia but can also be a double-edged sword. For example, using Black language in a job interview can cause you to miss out on the job opportunity. They don't think about things like Black Linguistic Justice but just want to see how professional you are. (Caleb Borketey)
>
> While growing up, I've even heard Black teachers tell Black students, "You sound very ignorant speaking that way. No one is going to hire you if you can't speak proper English." It is the sad truth, but writing a cover letter for your dream job is already extremely hard to do for Black Americans, for we are already being judged harder than our white opponents. (Jada Burroughs)

The apprehension of my students regarding the exclusion of Black language in the job market resonated with our shared concern as English faculty members at EWU. As instructors of English at an HBCU, we frequently engage in conversations on the significance of advocating for Black Linguistic Justice and endorsing our students' own languages. Nevertheless, we are also confronted with the obstacle of external influences and prevailing societal conventions, such as employment prospects that still prioritize a strict hierarchy of languages or educational settings where other instructors exclusively recognize Standard English as the only appropriate form of academic language. In this context, teaching and promoting the use of Black language to our students may be irresponsible, as it could potentially hinder their opportunities of securing better employment or achieving higher grades. This is particularly relevant considering that the majority of our students are first-generation and seek education to enhance their chances of accessing promising opportunities. Hence, teachers frequently encounter a predicament in which we must balance our inclination to promote racial equity with the practical considerations that would ultimately benefit our students.

As a teacher, I must navigate the constraints of a challenging reality while also striving to foster critical awareness. Consequently, I continue to instruct my students on crafting a "formal" professional cover letter and CV as part of their first-year writing projects. Simultaneously, I challenge them to explore the politics of "appropriate" language in their cover letters. Within this framework, I tasked my students with finding and developing their own research agenda and project about Black Linguistic Justice. For this purpose, I asked students to write a research proposal explaining their personal experiences speaking and writing Black in non-academic or academic spaces, as well as how these experiences related to their own research project. By reflecting their previous experiences with theoretical frameworks and in-class debates we had throughout the semester, I hoped my students would acknowledge that mainstream language practices lack the capacity to fully capture the experience and cultural knowledge of Black language speakers; therefore, their research should contribute to understanding the systemic racism in linguistics in their own projects.

The research papers they wrote were exceptionally captivating and creative. Most importantly, many students opted to create an independent project that establishes a connection between the notion of Black Linguistic Justice and a subject matter that holds great interest to them in their daily lives. For instance, Kwamon McGhee's project, titled "Exploring Black Linguistic Expression in Anime: Black Characters in *Naruto*," analyzed the speech patterns of Black characters in the Japanese anime *Naruto*. He examined the convergence of race and language in *Naruto*, which had a significant impact on global audiences. His analysis mostly centered on the portrayal of Black characters, examining how these characters communicate and express their Black identity through their speech patterns and bodily gestures. Dauntevian Williams examined his elementary school English textbook to comprehend the use and portrayal of Black language. He contended that Black children face close examination in an educational setting that is biased against them, and consequently, they experience linguistic challenges in the early stages of education and are disadvantaged due to their language. Akyma David, the winner of the 2023 Miss Edward Waters University pageant, conducted a study on the vocabulary used to describe Black beauty and pageants. She argued that Black beauty was characterized using both prejudiced and objectifying language by both Black and non-Black communities. Finally, Kayla M. Saunders, a Black female soccer player, analyzed the language employed by the mainstream media when describing Black female athletes.

The inclusion of Black Linguistic Justice in a composition course was evident in these stimulating projects, which effectively connect academic learning with real-world application for my students. The transformative potential of civic education in composition courses at HBCUs resides in its ability to empower students as agents of change and champions for social justice within our institutions.

Through the practice of engaging in discussion centered around Black Linguistic Justice, my students develop skills to effectively negotiate the many social challenges present in contemporary higher educational institutions, which reflects the spirit of community and collective action that has always defined the HBCU experience.

Conclusion

At the end of the semester, I reassigned my class the statement on Black Linguistic Justice and inquired whether their perception of Black language in academia and their understanding of their role in civic education had been altered in any way as a result of the course. My students exhibited their recognition of the significance of incorporating Black Linguistic Justice for Black students and that Standard English is not the only way to learn. Many of my students advocated for the creation of a "safe space for Black language in academia," which they believed could be initiated by the teacher, who is expected to "teach the way they want and therefore has the power to include linguistic justice in their lesson plan" (Kwamon McGhee). This implies that my students often had negative experiences engaging with their K–12 English teachers, who lacked understanding of Black students' language and often considered it inappropriate in the classroom. Thus, students consistently emphasized in their reflection essays the significance of Black Linguistic Justice in early education, stating that Black English "establishes during a Black child's most crucial learning and development years" (Kwamon KcGhee).

In this context, I would like to encourage my fellow teachers to include linguistic justice on their pedagogical agenda as soon as possible. I found that long-term exclusion from public education has left my students traumatized and ashamed of their language. As a non-native English speaker and non-Black minority teacher who does not speak Black English, I do not think that mastery of Black language is the essential condition to teach Black Linguistic Justice to Black students and others, since what matters more is the act of listening to students' real voices and respecting their languages.

The integration of civic education into composition courses at HBCUs holds immense potential for empowering students as informed, engaged citizens and advancing the institutions' missions of social justice and community engagement. By grounding course content in Black Linguistic Justice, my course fostered critical thinking, civic literacy, and social responsibility among students. HBCUs can continue to serve as catalysts for positive social change and democratic renewal, inspiring future generations to become active participants in democracy and advocates for equity and justice. This transformative impact extends beyond the classroom walls, shaping the civic identity and collective ethos of HBCU campuses, and making civic education more accessible and meaningful for students.

Works Cited

Allen, G. (2024, March 15). *Gov. Ron DeSantis' war on "woke" appears to be losing steam in Florida.* NPR. www.npr.org/2024/03/15/1238272873/desantis-woke-dont-say-gay-florida-stop-woke#:~:text=It%20marked%20the%20beginning%20of,race%2C%20sex%20or%20national%20origin

Baker-Bell, A., & Kynard, C. (2024). *#BlackLanguageSyllabus*. Black Linguistic Justice. wwwblacklanguagesyllabus.com/

Baker-Bell, A., Williams-Farrier, B., Jackson, D., Johnson, L., Kynard, C., & McMurtry, T. (2020). *This ain't another statement! This is a demand for Black Linguistic Justice!* Conference on College Composition and Communication. https://cccc.ncte.org/cccc/demand-for-black-linguistic-justice

Brown, M. C., & Dancy, T. E. (Eds.). (2017). *Black colleges across the diaspora: Global perspectives on race and stratification in postsecondary education.* Emerald Publishing.

Cokley, K. (2002). The impact of college racial composition on African American students' academic self-concept: A replication and extension. *The Journal of Negro Education, 71*(4), 288–296.

DeSantis, R. [GovRonDeSantis]. (2021, June 10). *Stop critical race theory in our schools* [Video]. Rumble. https://rumble.com/vicrc3-stop-critical-race-theory-in-our-schools.html

Florida Department of Education. (2021, December 27). *2021 Florida Department of Education major accomplishments.* www.fldoe.org/newsroom/latest-news/2021-florida-department-of-education-major-accomplishments.stml

Hutchinson, B., & Wash, S. (2023, August 28). *Security guard details encounter with alleged Jacksonville gunman prior to racially motivated shooting.* ABC News. https://abcnews.go.com/US/security-guard-details-encounter-alleged-jacksonville-gunman-prior/story?id=102617339

Osorio, N. (2022, July 7). *UCF's English department suspends anti-racism statement following the passage of Stop WOKE Act in Florida.* Orlando Weekly. www.orlandoweekly.com/news/ucfs-english-department-suspends-anti-racism-statement-following-the-passage-of-stop-woke-act-in-florida-31978303

Stepzinski, T. (2023, August 26). 3 Black victims killed in racially motivated shooting at Jacksonville Dollar General. *The Florida Times-Union.* www.jacksonville.com/story/news/crime/2023/08/26/fatal-shooting-reported-near-edward-waters-university-dollar-general-kings-road-jacksonville/70690958007/

Tingle, N. H. (2021). *Doin' it for the culture: An exploration of critical consciousness and civic engagement within HBCU core curriculum* [Doctoral dissertation, Auburn University]. AUETD.

SECTION 3
The Ins and Outs of Teaching for Civic Engagement

Asian American Civic Inquiry in Action in the Secondary ELA Classroom

MINKYUNG CHOI, DIANA LIU & JEAN KIM

Introduction

Given the dearth of Asian American (AsAm) histories, stories, and experiences in K–12 curricula, mandates like the Teaching Equitable Asian American Community History (TEAACH) Act in Illinois are pivotal in increasing representation. While these mandates are critical in that they recognize the importance of AsAm stories and histories, they raise several questions about the practices surrounding them. For instance, is attention given to expanding dominant narratives of Asians as passive victims or as threats? Are notions of civic engagement being reimagined to align more closely with Asian American students' life experiences (Rodríguez & Kim, 2018)? Are teachers critically engaging in this work by placing narratives in more complex sociocultural and political contexts?

Inextricably woven into these questions are issues surrounding power and criticality. As such, we, as Asian American female educators, critically examine the pedagogical practices of our educational spaces when centering AsAm identities. Min is a researcher and assistant professor in a teacher education program, Diana is a full-time NYC DOE high school English teacher in Brooklyn and an English Education PhD candidate, and Jean is a full-time NYC DOE middle school English teacher in Queens. The three of us met through a summer educator workshop titled "Teacher-Led Instruction: Creating Asian American & Pacific Islander Curriculum." In this essay, we consider how teachers can incorporate AsAm literature to increase civic inquiry for all students.

The power of literature as a conduit for drawing students into new, unexplored worlds is well documented, but perhaps less explicit is the connection between English classrooms and civic education, which is frequently reduced to a narrow perspective that emphasizes discussions on adhering to the law and voting (Westheimer & Kahne, 2004). Authentic civic learning necessitates a more profound and personal development of *critical civic empathy*—"embodying the lives of our fellow citizens while keeping in mind the social forces that differentiate our experiences as we make decisions about our shared public future" (Mirra, 2018, p. 7). Critical civic empathy can be developed when teachers select texts that challenge and extend students' identities and experiences and, more importantly, intentionally structure essential questions and activities that do so (Mirra, 2018).

The motivation for this essay is not necessarily to define one set approach to using AsAm literature to engage students in civic inquiry but rather to extend an invitation to reimagine ways in which teaching and reading AsAm literature in the secondary English classroom can be a site for civic inquiry to flourish.

What Kind of Citizens?

The three of us met through a summer educator workshop titled "Teacher-Led Instruction: Creating Asian American & Pacific Islander Curriculum," during which we designed the lesson plans described in this paper. We use the title of an article published by Westheimer and Kahne (2004) here to reflect on the end goal of the kind of civic action that the lesson plans encourage. In the article, Westheimer and Kahne (2004) categorize three kinds of citizens: personally responsible citizens, participatory citizens, and justice-oriented citizens. Simply put, personally responsible citizens act responsibly in their communities through acts of picking up trash or volunteering. Participatory citizens are described as those who are actively involved in community organizations and are familiar with the functions of various government organizations. Justice-oriented citizens, by contrast, may not seem to take observable action, but they critically question systemic structures that contribute to inequities. The authors point out that justice-oriented citizenship is least commonly pursued in curricula but is of critical importance.

The lesson plans that were created strived to advance frameworks that develop justice-oriented citizens by engaging students in "informed analysis and discussion regarding social, political, and economic structures" and encouraging them to consider "collective strategies for change that challenge injustice and, when possible, address root causes of the problem" (Westheimer & Kahne, 2004, p. 242). As such, they challenge educators to shift the way in which we conceptualize civic action to include transformative thinking and questioning.

We come together as a collective of Asian American female educators to critically examine the pedagogical practices of our respective educational spaces when we center AsAm identities and voices.

Where Civic Inquiry Begins

Something that came up in discussions both during and after the professional development workshop was the need for different frameworks when thinking about developing AsAm curriculum. So often, AsAm history is taught (*when* it is taught) as isolated events and through a Eurocentric, colonist lens, and what this does is depict Asian Americans as victims or threats. Nowhere are Asian Americans seen as resilient individuals who have agency or as working in collaboration with other communities. What's missing is an AsAm-centered framework, one that centers civic inquiry and action. The professional development workshop introduced an AsAm-centered framework, asking questions that pointed to some of the concerns and issues that have been raised with regard to AsAm history. This was helpful for us in thinking about how to anchor our lesson plans and how to ensure we weren't adding to the pervasive harmful narratives. We revised some of the categories to make stronger connections to civic inquiry and action.

Framework

Ethnic Studies

We draw from ethnic studies methodologies as defined by Agarwal-Rangath (2020) and Yeh et al. (2021a) where the goals are: "1) rehumanizing educational experiences for our youth; 2) acknowledging the histories, resilience, and resistance of communities of color; and 3)

Table 1

AAPI-Centered Lens *(developed by the Asian American Education Project)*	**AsAm-Centered Lens with Civic Inquiry & Action**
Does my lesson teach about AAPI histories or narratives from the perspective of an AAPI person? (Does the lesson include perspectives from AAPI people and/or communities? Does this lesson reject and/or challenge the dominant white perspective about this community?)	Does my lesson teach about AsAm activist histories and narratives from the perspective of an AsAm person? Does my lesson feature AsAm activist solidarity with other communities of color and white allyship? (Does the lesson include perspectives from AsAm people and/or communities? Does this lesson reject and/or challenge the dominant white perspective about this community?)
Does my lesson center resistance, joy, or agency in some way? (Does my lesson go beyond just focusing on oppression and what has happened to this community?)	Does my lesson center the ongoing resistance, joy, and agency of AsAm people and its communities? (Does my lesson go beyond just focusing on overcoming historical oppressions and what has happened to the various communities and instead emphasize continuous engagement?)
How am I ensuring that this community is not seen as a monolith? (Which AAPI community am I representing? Why? How?)	How am I ensuring the intersectional identities of AsAm communities so that the communities are not seen as monoliths? How do I represent the interconnectedness of AsAm communities with others? Why? How?

shifting the use of education from awareness to action" (p. 3). By centering and leaning on such tenets of ethnic studies, we are able to recenter histories and identities of people of color and disrupt white supremacy and colonial effects within the curriculum at the secondary level.

Multiplicity and Asian American Feminist Praxis

We also draw from Asian American feminist theory that highlights the importance of considering the intersections of race and gender when considering Asian American women and their contexts (Hsieh and Nguyen, 2020). As a collective, we seek to "unpack overlapping injustices based on the gendered and racialized contexts in which AsAm women exist" and how these injustices unfold in the way we design our lesson plans and engage in our pedagogical practices in classrooms (Hsieh & Ngyuen, 2020, p. 356).

Furthermore, this lens of multiplicity allows us to critically examine our conceptions of solidarity that allow for bringing people together through acknowledging oppression through lived experiences but also holding each other accountable for the varied power and privileges that we have (Fujiwara &

Roshanravan, 2018). At the same time, we need to practice naming differences within Asian America when engaging with solidarity, or else we risk reinforcing Asian Americans as invisible coalitional agents with other communities of color (Fujiwara & Roshanravan, 2018).

Lowe (1991) states, "An Asian American subject is never purely and exclusively ethnic, for that subject is always of a particular class, gender, and sexual preference and may therefore feel responsible to movements that are organized around these designations . . . [T]hese differences represent greater political opportunity to affiliate with other groups whose cohesions may be based on other valences of oppression" (p. 32). As a result, we must also acknowledge the way our own positions as Asian American female educators inform the way we teach and examine our lesson plans that acknowledge the varied intersections of race, gender, and class in different ways.

What Does Civic Action Look Like From Teaching the Lesson Plans?

An analysis of the lesson plans revealed that civic action necessitates a willingness to learn about the history and culture of diverse Asian communities by sharing each other's narratives. The teaching of AsAm stories not only "eliminate[s] conflict and group differences in ways that privilege those in power and continue to oppress subordinate groups" but also addresses the "need for collective identifications" (Mirra & Morrell, 2011). In addition, by offering students a breadth of stories both about and written by Asian American authors, teachers can challenge the misconception that Asian Americans are "silent" and emphasize that Asians, too, are an integral part of America. The following lesson plans highlight how two teachers, Jean and Diana, created ELA lesson plans that explore how AsAm stories can be taught in ways that develop students' civic inquiry and action. Resources associated with these lessons can be found at https://bit.ly/NCTECivics.

Jean: Teaching *Dragonwings* by Laurence Yep

The *Dragonwings* unit was taught to sixth graders in a public middle school in Queens, New York. The school is 74 percent minority enrollment, where the majority of the students are Asian/Asian American. I generally teach the unit toward the end of the school year to ensure students understand the importance of broadening narratives by sharing their own. By this point of the year, students are familiar with sharing their personal experience and how this practice reduces misconceptions and misunderstandings of each other. *Dragonwings* is an ideal book to elaborate the significance of this practice as the main plot revolves around the initial conflict between characters due to stereotypical perceptions. As the story progresses, the characters grow closer, breaking down the stereotypes they had by sharing and understanding each other's stories. The story also shows how the main character dreams of flying with his own airplane, challenging stereotypes of Asian immigrants as being submissive and solely focused on education.

As a prereading activity, students delve into the historical context of the text by creating historical background slides on an assigned topic. In groups, students research their assigned topics and deliver a short presentation, leaving the audience with thought-provoking questions. These group presentations not only help students have a better understanding of the plot but deepen their knowledge of the early years of Chinese American history. Although, as mentioned above, the Chinese Exclusion Act is one of the two major events that are covered in social studies curricula, it's surprising to see how few Asian, even Chinese, students know about the act. Students can be active learners about the beginning of Chinese immigration by conducting their own research. Moreover, some of the suggested topics encourage students to explore Chinese immigration from other perspectives, enabling them to also learn about the "resilience, agency, and advocacy" of Chinese immigrants "in the face of oppression" they confronted under the Chinese Exclusion Act, which is normally the dominant theme discussed (Heish & Kim, 2020). After the presentations, students complete a reflection worksheet, sharing what they newly learned and making connections between the text and broader cultural issues (text-to-world connections), as well as relating the text to their personal experiences (text-to-self connections).

The prereading activity allowed students to discuss the different layers of early Chinese American history. For instance, one group elaborated on the contributions Asian immigrants made in the early 1900s, highlighting Asian Americans as integral parts of American history. These discussions are crucial for Asian American students as there is a cultural tendency to "erase the contributions of Asian Americans throughout history to the development of the United States (Goodwin, 2010; Ng et al., 2007), perpetually casting them as a culturally distinct population living in America" (Hsieh & Kim, 2020).

Another group delivered a presentation on China in the 1900s, explaining the struggles Chinese people went through that compelled some to risk their lives by immigrating to other countries, including America. Students then naturally discussed the struggles Chinese immigrants must have experienced being foreigners in a country they needed to consider as their home. The final questions students left were focused more on how the Chinese immigrants would have felt at that moment, which organically helped students increase their civic empathy toward immigrants.

One group's presentation on immigrant women highlighted how their rights were more restricted compared to those of their male counterparts, a point that resonates with the limited representation of female Chinese characters in the story. This observation sparked meaningful discussions about women's roles in the 1900s, emphasizing how the female characters in the narrative were predominantly passive. These insights also underscored the broader issue of limited female agency in the story.

Delving deeper into civic empathy, students were able to make meaningful text-to-self connections through the reflection worksheet debrief. Given that most of my students came from immigrant families, with half of the school's population being Asian Americans, I was particularly interested to hear how they related to the historical background of *Dragonwings*. It was especially significant to give students space to learn and share about their ethnic group's first experience of America and how it was similar and different from the Chinese Americans. According to Hsieh and Kim, "Asian Americans are almost universally lumped together as being similar in culture" along with their histories in the States (2020). As a result, "there is little recognition of the ways in which Asian Americans from distinct ethnic subgroups within the Asian diaspora may struggle with stereotypes, histories, and other experiences unique to them" (2020). By sharing the diverse historical narratives as a community, students engaged in a rich conversation regarding how each ethnic group possessed distinctive historical backgrounds while also experiencing similar emotions and difficulties that they endured as foreigners.

Overall, the prereading activity helped students acknowledge the extensive history of Asian Americans, challenging the entrenched stereotype of Asians as being "forever foreigners" who are "always first-generation immigrants, new to the United States" (Hsieh & Kim, 2020, p. 97). Additionally, the activity enhanced the understanding of Asian American history among non-Asian students as well, prompting them to recognize that "the history of America includes Asian Americans" (Hsieh & Kim, 2020).

Diana: Teaching *Anger Is a Gift* by Mark Oshiro

This unit was taught to ninth graders in a public high school in Brooklyn, New York. The school is 77.3 percent minority enrollment, where the majority of the students are Asian/Asian American. When teaching *Anger Is a Gift* by Mark Oshiro, I focused on this text featuring Moss, who embodies a layering of identities including one as a Black gay youth. The text also focuses on many social issues such as mental health/trauma, LGBTQIA+ experiences as a person of color, gentrification, inequities across race, socioeconomic class, police brutality, ableism, racism, and more through the main character Moss and the community around him.

This is usually one of the last units taught in the academic year because throughout the year, students are consistently unpacking their identities through the other designed units. We do this in order to co-construct a classroom space that invites dialogue and critical self-reflection that unpacks our racial literacies so we can build understanding, empathy, and action (Sealey-Ruiz, 2022). When we approach the *Anger Is a Gift* unit, students have been used to navigating some difficult topics and unpacking their identities and are ready to take it a step further.

During this unit, students begin to examine the setting of Oakland, California, through its socioeconomic landscape. We also delve into the history and references of Oscar Grant III, the backdrop in which Moss begins to encounter protests against police brutality. Although this text is not centered on Asian American identities, I create space for students of mine who are predominantly Asian American to grapple with the differences. Through the text, we continue to discuss and have students draw personal connections to the inequities in the book to ones they observe around New York City. Furthermore, students examine power dynamics between characters and systems through characterization and drama activities in the form of monologues during their previous unit to discuss the relations of identities, privileges, and power dynamics. Without modeling and guiding students in discussions to talk about such topics and how they themselves are within these systems, "we cannot begin the dialogue needed to address the big problems we collectively face" (Mirra, 2020, p. 10).

Students continue to extend their examination of the way Moss engages in activism by analyzing the ways Asian American communities engage in activism in solidarity with Black communities to build critical literacy skills and activism through social media. Much of what happens in Moss's school is spread through social media. The unit works toward our summative assessment, as students investigate a social issue within their own community and analyze the issue through a variety of lenses in order to develop a tangible "first-step" solution. Many social issues revolve around an imbalance in power structures and privileges, so students will be able to apply what they observe in the novel to observing any power imbalances they see in their own lives and communities.

As Mirra and Morrell (2011) note, "[this acknowledgment of educational inequalities] starts with recognition that these race-based inequalities are being manifested within a specific social context characterized by systemic inequality—one that allocates disproportionate economic, political, social, and academic rewards to a dominant White majority while structurally and culturally marginalizing communities of color" (as Bonilla-Silva notes in Mira & Morrell, 2011, p. 411).

Who Do We See as Activists?

When I begin asking students who they know as activists and what it means to be an activist, students are often able to name Martin Luther King Jr. and, occasionally, some students might name Malcolm X. Yet there is a noticeable pause of silence as I observe students furrow their brows to think of anyone else they could name. I never had my ninth-grade students on their own be able to name an Asian American activist yet. Through one of the videos I show students titled "Youa Vang Lee mourns George Floyd" from the May 19 Project by Renee Tajima-Peña and Jeff Chang, we begin our discussions of this more recent example as belonging to a long history of Asian American activism. Especially through this example, I emphasize the often-unacknowledged roles that strong women and mothers play in their identities as activists and piece our discussions with "The Transformation of Silence into Action" by Audre Lorde. These discussions at the intersection of gender, social class, and race allow students a deeper understanding and unpacking at a more systemic level of power and oppression that connect to the character, Moss, and ultimately how, through his mother and community's support, anger becomes a powerful and transformative emotion for social change.

As an educator, it is also my responsibility to teach that even the term "Asian American" has a unique activist history. Inspired by Black, Chicanx, and Indigenous civil rights movements during the 1960s, Emma Gee and Yuji Ichioka coined the term Asian American, "a diverse, multiethnic group united by politics aimed at ending oppression and inequality in the United States" (Maeda, 2012, as cited in Rodríguez & Kim, 2018, p. 18). By navigating these often-difficult conversations about race, power, and privilege with my students and building these kinds of critical connections with our students, "we have the opportunity to structure our practice in ways that foster relationships among the students in front of us and with the broader global community—to help students see themselves as part of collectives larger than themselves with whom they must collaborate" (Mirra, 2020, p. 11).

Next Steps

An analysis of the lesson plans revealed three ways the AsAm-centered lessons might foster critical civic empathy. First, they presented a multiplicity of identities through Asian characters that interrupted negative stereotypes of Asian American identity as a monolith, as passive and vulnerable. The lessons asked students to consider how narrative plentitude and scarcity shape perceptions of others and how the power of storytelling impacts the way personal histories are (re)constructed and how it creates spaces for imaginative possibilities (Nguyen, 2018). Second, they highlighted solidarity between AsAm communities and other communities of color in movements of resistance.

Reflecting as scholar-educators through class and after-school discussions, many of Jean and Diana's students recognized white supremacy as the root of oppression of racial groups rather than each other. Many of the students questioned why there were so many important pieces of history being left out of their education, and they agreed on the need to learn each other's history and to challenge dominant perspectives about an absence of solidarities among groups, and they further emphasized teachers' responsibilities to teach and make space in the curriculum for the skills of media literacy. Ultimately, students also agreed with the idea that "change starts with the self and the community around you" and began to brainstorm what that would look like at our school. As one female student writes in her reflection on solidarity:

> Solidarity can be reserved within the quainter corners of collaboration through founded kinship. Solidarity is the anticipation of communal inclusion, whether it is what fuels a united front against divisive impediments or an unadorned thread of yarn tying together two individuals.

Literary works introduced through a framework of thick solidarity, which is a thickness that can withstand critique and ". . . layers interpersonal empathy with historical analysis, political acumen, and a willingness to be led by those most directly impacted" (Liu & Shange, 2018, p. 196), demonstrated the importance of historical understanding, analysis, and collaboration in enacting systemic change. To engage in moving toward thick solidarity requires teachers to begin mindfully pairing texts with conversation and help students unpack the historical and systemic contexts behind ideas as well as to "mine" and "mind" the tensions that exist between groups. This means being comfortable having uncomfortable conversations such as how colorism and the model minority myth play roles in perpetuating inter- and intragroup racism.

Third, a dialogic process of examining novels and stories reflected how racial prejudice contributes to the social, political, and legislative marginalization of AsAm groups. The literary texts and instructional activities included in the lesson plans were guided by essential questions and enduring understandings that sought to deepen understandings of AsAm communities that have long been overlooked. While the study focused on AsAm histories, the implications for engaging students' critical civic empathy transcend AsAm communities—critical civic empathy allows us to imagine possibilities of a shared future.

Resources for the lessons described here can be found at https://bit.ly/NCTECivics.

Works Cited

Budiman, A., & Ruiz, N. G. (2021, April 9). *Asian Americans are the fastest-growing racial or ethnic group in the U.S.* Pew Research Center. www.pewresearch.org/fact-tank/2021/04/09/asian-americans-are-the-fastest-growing-racial-or-ethnic-group-in-the-u-s/

Fujiwara, L., & Roshanravan, S. (Eds.). (2018). *Asian American feminisms and women of color politics.* University of Washington Press.

Hsieh, B., & Kim, J. (2020). Challenging the invisibility of Asian Americans in education. *Review of Education, Pedagogy, and Cultural Studies, 42*(2), 95–103.

Hsieh, B., & Nguyen, H. T. (2020). Identity-informed mentoring to support acculturation of female faculty of color in higher education: An Asian American female mentoring relationship case study. *Journal of Diversity in Higher Education, 13*(2), 169.

Liu, R., & Shange, S. (2018). Toward thick solidarity: Theorizing empathy in social justice movements. *Radical History Review, 2018*(131), 189–198. https://doi.org/10.1215/01636545-4355341

Lowe, L. (1991). Heterogeneity, hybridity, multiplicity: Marking Asian American differences. *Diaspora: A Journal of Transnational Studies, 1*(1), 24–44.

Mirra, N. (2018). *Educating for empathy: Literacy learning and civic engagement.* Teachers College Press.

Mirra, N. (2020). A quality of imagination: Young people show us "what's next" in ELA. *Voices from the Middle, 27*(4), 9–11. http://ezproxy.cul.columbia.edu/login?url=https://www.proquest.com/scholarly-journals/quality-imagination-young-people-show-us-whats/docview/2417395909/se-2

Mirra, N., & Morrell, E. (2011). Teachers as civic agents: Toward a critical democratic theory of urban teacher development. *Journal of Teacher Education, 62*(4), 408–420. https://link-gale-com.ezproxy.cul.columbia.edu/apps/doc/A266629719/BIC?u=columbiau&sid=summon&xid=aac1009d

Nguyen, V. T. (2018, December 19). *Narrative plentitude with Viet Thanh Nguyen and Vu Tran: Talks at Google* [Video]. YouTube. www.youtube.com/watch?v=gqiPoZOy3VE

Rodriguez, N. N., & Kim, E. J. (2018). In search of mirrors: An Asian critical race theory content analysis of Asian American picturebooks from 2007 to 2017 *Journal of Children's Literature, 44*(2), 17–30. www.childrensliteratureassembly.org/uploads/1/1/8/6/118631535/in_search_of_mirrors_an_asian_critical_race_theory_content_analysis_of_asian_american_picturebooks_from_2007_to_2017.pdf

Sealey-Ruiz, Y. (2022). An Archaeology of Self for our times: Another talk to teachers. *English Journal, 111*(5), 21–26. https://doi.org/10.58680/ej202231819

Westheimer, J., & Kahne, J. (2004). Educating the "good" citizen: Political choices and pedagogical goals. *PS: Political Science & Politics, 37*(2), 241–247.

Westheimer, J., & Kahne, J. (2004). What kind of citizen? The politics of educating for democracy. *American Educational Research Journal, 41*(2), 237–269.

Yeh, C., Agarwal-Rangnath, R., & Albarran Moses, A. (2023). Abolition and ethnic studies in early care and education. *Contemporary Issues in Early Childhood, 24*(2), 208–225. https://doi-org.ezproxy.cul.columbia.edu/10.1177/14639491231165291

Civic Engagement in the Here and Now: Conversational Moves for Democratic Participation

KARLA ZACCOR

I'm teaching you this stuff so you can change it. Not just so you can be smart and impress your friends with how much you know about the world.
—Kurian Joseph[1], high school US history teacher

Classrooms must be more than places where we simply learn about civic engagement and how it should occur in the world; they must be places where we actively practice civic engagement or, as Shalaby (2017) says, "places in which we practice freedom" (p. xvi). In this way, practice means both "way of living out" and "continually improving." Traditional civics education focuses on teaching students about our democratic institutions through a collection of facts and events to be memorized rather than helping students develop tools to interrogate problems that impact their lives (Mirra & Garcia, 2022). Instead of traditional approaches, I take up Mirra and Garcia's (2022) reframing of civics education as a practice of "leveraging students' everyday realities as the catalyst for understanding democratic norms and institutions" (p. 350).

Specifically, in this chapter, I argue we need *civic practices* in classrooms. To delineate civic practices in the context of classroom talk, I focus on analyzing conversational moves in classroom discussions. After all, the ways teachers pose questions and respond to student contributions impact how students are positioned as members of the classroom community, thereby creating conditions for civic practices. My central research question here is: *What conversational moves does a teacher employ that create opportunities for the practice of civic engagement within the classroom?* To answer this, I use reconstructive discourse analysis (Luke, 2004; Taylor & Hikida, 2023) to examine discourse between students and teacher in a high school classroom, examining dialogue as a way for enacting a practice of civic engagement. In this way, discursive moves can be seen as civic practices that create classroom communities that are microcosms of the world we want: a world where everyone is safe and taken care of, where problems are addressed, where we practice freedom. Rather than viewing schooling solely as preparation for a future life of democratic citizenship, I look at the classroom as a site of civic engagement for the here and now.

Classroom Context

I collected classroom observation data for a larger project in a tenth-grade US history class in

1. All people and place names other than the city of Chicago are pseudonyms.

a public school in Chicago during the 2014–2015 school year. At the time of data collection, Mandela High School had 308 students in grades 9–12. According to the district website, the student demographics at the time were 81.8 percent Black, 11 percent Hispanic, 2.6 percent white, 2.3 percent Asian, and 2.3 percent other. A total of 95.8 percent of the students were considered low income, 24.4 percent received special education services, and 7.1 percent were considered limited English proficient. I spent four months observing in two periods of Kurian Joseph's sophomore US history class—one class had 30 students and the other class had 32 students. Kurian is of South Indian descent and was in his tenth year of teaching. During this school year, the world handed us plenty of curriculum (Ahmed, 2018; more on this below). As we will see, Kurian taught his curriculum so that students' "civic expertise" outside of school was relevant and solicited.

Kurian's US History Curriculum

Kurian created a list of essential questions that aligned with the unit topics for his tenth-grade US history curriculum. (To access the list, go to https://bit.ly/NCTECivics). We see from the overview that Kurian took a non-traditional approach to teaching US history. The essential questions demonstrate the critical perspective Kurian aimed for. He designed his curriculum so students could see the through line from history to today, with a focus on the ways racism and oppression are endemic to the United States (see Zaccor, 2022). During the time I was there, they explored units on mass incarceration, income inequality, and violence in Chicago, all issues students faced on a regular basis. Before Kurian began his unit on mass incarceration, for example, he gave his students a survey asking if they had someone in their family and/or someone they are close to who had been in the prison system. Over ninety percent of the students said yes to both questions, a clear indication that these issues were grounded in their lives.

Civic Engagement during Classroom Discussions

In Kurian's classroom, civic engagement was facilitated by 1) the content and structure of his curriculum/units of study, including the texts they learned from, and 2) how he facilitated classroom discussion. I will highlight two examples from Kurian's classroom that illustrate how both aspects fostered civic participation.

Beyond the Idea of a Singular Correctness

In the first example, the class was in the middle of the unit on the Gilded Age and economic inequality. The objective for this day's lesson was: Identify pro- and anti-capitalist views. To do this, Kurian shared excerpts written by four different people (e.g., an excerpt from Andrew Carnegie's *Wealth and Its Uses*), and the students were to identify the excerpt as pro- or anti-capitalist and explain why. The students were completing the sheet that guides them through this work, and Kurian was circulating. Here is an excerpt from my field notes during the lesson:

> Jada is having a hard time understanding what the bees and honey are a metaphor for; Kurian asks if someone can explain it to her. A couple students chime in to say that the honey is a metaphor for money and the bees are the capitalists. Kurian says, "Okay, let's read number three together." Tamera starts reading the excerpt and mispronounces "ought to." Kurian corrects her quickly and Tamera responds "ohhhhh" (like she didn't realize that was how it was spelled). Kurian quickly adds, "It's old, nobody really talks like that anymore." Jeremiah laughs at Tamera's mispronunciation and Kurian

says, "Nobody here is perfect." He then tells Tamera to "keep reading, don't let people keep you down" (a joking response to Jeremiah laughing). Tamera continues reading. Another student interrupts, "What does shortcomings mean?" and Kurian answers, "Weaknesses; things you're not good at." When Tamera finishes reading the excerpt, Kurian asks the class, "Is the person for it or against it?" A chorus of students say "For." Jeremiah says the person who wrote the excerpt sounds like a poor person for capitalism because "he keeps writing they, they, they instead of we, we, we." Kurian agrees and points to the part in the text where it says the author is a reverend and adds, "So, he might not be poor, but he's not a capitalist." Kurian points out that the excerpt says poor people are poor because it's their fault and reminds them of the graphic they looked at the other day that illustrated people climbing up a ladder. He reminds them to write their answers on the sheet for number 3: "How does he feel about rich people?" Jeremiah answers, "They're trustable, honest." Tinesha says, "Trustable?" and Kurian, ignoring Tinesha and responding to Jeremiah's comment, says, "Yeah, [he's saying] they're the most honest people in our society." A couple kids are still repeating trustable and someone asks, "Is that a word?" Kurian laughs and says, "Trustworthy is the word" and says under his breath that the students aren't letting anything go today. He tells them, "Once you memorize the dictionary you can use words how you want."

In thinking about the ways Kurian fosters discussion, there are a few things worth highlighting from this example of classroom talk. Kurian created opportunities for students to share knowledge and build understanding together. First, Jada felt comfortable saying that she was confused by what the metaphor was saying about capitalism. Kurian's response illustrates that it is okay to not understand something and also that students should help each other. This happened other times when students had questions about particular words. When Jada mispronounced "ought to," another student asked what shortcomings means, and Jeremiah used "trustable," Kurian's responses again showed that small mistakes or misunderstandings are normal and even expected. He did not position students as lacking; he used reassuring language ("nobody really talks like that anymore") to emphasize that Jada made a mistake that anyone could make. He also centered students' language as normal and this other way of using language as unusual. He even tried to roll with Jeremiah's use of trustable; it wasn't until students repeatedly called attention to the word that he again used reassuring language when he said "once you memorize the dictionary you can use words how you want."

In an educational system where getting correct answers is a gatekeeping mechanism, Kurian's willingness to accept approximations demonstrated his focus on students' own knowledge and their developing understandings of bigger picture ideas. These kinds of responses were typical of Kurian's back and forth with students. For example, on another day they were reviewing for the upcoming Constitution test and Jada answered "elderman" instead of "alderman" in response to a question about who was elected to city council in each ward in Chicago. Kurian corrected her saying, "But that was close" (to which Jeremiah exclaimed, "Don't lie to her, bro!").

There was a negotiation happening in the classroom (between students, mostly) about what "counts" as acceptable contributions to a discussion. Kurian allowed these multiple positions to co-occur without shutting down students—even if he erred slightly on the side of allowing wider use of language than the strict grammarians in the classroom wanted—as one mechanism for pushing back on this dominant idea of "correct" or "one right way." Students knew they did not need their comments to be within a narrow frame of "acceptable" discourse practices, which allowed for more democratic participation. This is an example of practicing civic literacies: keeping the focus on the content of students' contributions rather than gatekeeping the form, thus allowing wider and more authentic participation.

Interrogating State-Sanctioned Violence

In November of 2014, a grand jury decided not to indict Darren Wilson for killing Michael Brown in Ferguson, Missouri. The next day, Kurian scrapped whatever plans he had and dedicated the class period to discussing the case. The bellringer for the day asked: "What do you know about last night's news related to the killing of Mike Brown in Ferguson?" After a couple volunteers shared out ("saw stuff on fire in Ferguson," "the officer was found not guilty," "not indicted"), Kurian said, "So, he wasn't found not guilty; that's from a trial. This was just a grand jury. It's made up of twelve people. I didn't know what a grand jury was until I started watching the news, and I looked it up. And so, I wanted to share it so we can make sense of what happened here." He then passed out handouts that described what a grand jury is.

Similar to the previous example, Kurian made it clear that it is normal to not be familiar with a grand jury. Where traditional narratives of schooling position an official body of knowledge as important things worth knowing and teachers having the responsibility of making students be "in the know" of this body of knowledge, Kurian instead acknowledges that prior to now, there was no real reason for him (nor the students) to know what a grand jury is. Now that there is a reason, he did some research, and now he wants to share that research with them. A traditional civics education might posit that students learn about grand juries when they read chapter 6 of their American civics textbook—in a manner that would be completely divorced from students' lived experiences. Here, Kurian was helping broaden their civic knowledge in a meaningful context. It was apparent that it was meaningful; students shushed each other so they could read the handouts in order to make sense of the injustice that had occurred the night before.

After more discussion about how a grand jury works and how many people think the non-indictment is unjust, this discussion happened:

> ***Kurian:*** *A lot of people are angry, right? So, I want to talk about how people are channeling their anger about this. It's not just a Ferguson, Missouri, problem. It's a Chicago problem, a New York problem, an LA problem.*
>
> ***Kendrell:*** *Why are there all these problems?*
>
> ***Kurian:*** *Yeah, so Kendrell's asking about the police violence. Like, the police are killing particularly Black males but Black females as well. All across the country, right? That's the million-dollar question—why? What's going on? It's obviously racism, right? But that's something we gotta figure out.*
>
> ***Kendrell:*** *Why do people say it's racist when we kill each other every day?*
>
> ***Kurian:*** *Wait, what are you talking about? You talking about Michael Brown getting shot?*
>
> ***Kendrell:*** *Yeah.*

> ***Kurian:*** *People are saying that's racist because the cop was white.*

There are two noteworthy things about this exchange. First, Kurian frames the problem of police violence as unequivocally racist, but also as something "we gotta figure out." This is similar to language he uses in the previous exchange where he tells them he brought information about the grand jury so "we can make sense of what happened." His use of "we" communicated a particular stance as a teacher—he did not take a position of "I know things, and I'm going to tell you what I know" but rather "I don't understand, either. Maybe we can reach an understanding together." Here, "reaching an understanding" is a deeper interrogation of how and why police are repeatedly killing Black people. Kurian's conversational moves show his students that he believes them to be capable of this level of analysis.

The other noteworthy thing is Kurian's refusal to let Kendrell shift the focus of the conversation to so-called Black-on-Black crime. His tone when he asked, "Wait, what are you talking about?" was one of genuine confusion at Kendrell's question. I don't know whether Kurian was actually confused or not, but he did not allow the focus of the conversation to deviate from police as perpetrators of violence against Black people. Whereas in other classroom discussions, Kurian was open to hearing students' perspectives, even if it shifted the conversation, in this conversation, he was not going to let the police off the hook. A similar thing happened a few minutes later when they were discussing news clips they had seen of protestors in Ferguson:

> ***Kurian:*** *The police aren't really helping the situation. Last night, the cops were out in their military gear, really just trying to intimidate people. People aren't out to destroy stuff; they're out to express their anger and protest, and this is the kind of response they're getting from the police [he puts pictures up of police in riot gear]. Did you guys hear about the protests in Chicago last night? They were on 35th and Michigan and then made their way to downtown. It was kind of a big crowd. They went on to Lake Shore Drive and were marching on Lake Shore Drive, shutting down traffic.*
>
> ***Davonte:*** *You seen that news reporter who got hit in the head with a rock? Somebody threw a rock at her head.*
>
> ***Kurian:*** *Wait, who got hit in the head?*
>
> ***Davonte:*** *The news reporter!*
>
> ***Kurian:*** *Oh, the news reporter. Yeah, I know the police have been shooting rubber bullets at protestors and stuff. So, some women and kids have been getting hit by the police out in Ferguson.*

Similarly, Kurian refused to let Davonte reframe the conversation. His response to Davonte's comment did not even match (rocks and rubber bullets), but Kurian was adamant about keeping the focus on the police's violent responses to protestors. In both cases, Kendrell and Davonte did not keep pushing their line of questioning. There might be a case to be made on hearing students out and trying to understand where they are coming from, but Kurian chose to keep state-sanctioned violence at the center of their discussion. What does that tell us about civic participation? Kurian is teaching them to engage the power structure, not repeat lines they hear in the media ("we kill each other every day"). Pursuing those lines of questioning would not have helped them "grapple with, analyze, and develop critical understandings" of their world (Clay & Rubin, 2019, p. 164).

In this example, Kurian is facilitating the practice of civic literacies by using the real world as the "text" for the day. Although Kurian had a tightly planned curriculum that often felt rushed (more on that in the next section), he also did not shy away from discussing current issues—because Kurian was creating opportunities for students to engage in the present world, not just preparing them for future civic participation. Several times that day and throughout the time I visited, Kurian emphasized, "I'm teaching you this stuff so you can change it. Not just so you can be smart and impress your friends with how much you know about the world."

What Kurian Teaches Us about Civic Engagement

Kurian engaged his students in civic practices through his critical US history curriculum and the ways he positioned his students as knowledgeable and his classroom as a space where knowledge was constructed together. To be clear, Kurian's classroom was not a utopian space. There were varying levels of engagement, and there were many days when class felt like a rush to complete an assignment rather than creating space for more in-depth dialogue and dreaming about civic futures (Mirra & Garcia, 2020; Garcia & Mirra, 2021). For example, one day during the unit on root causes of violence in Chicago, the bellringer for the day was: *Is it possible for people to make governments actually help struggling neighborhoods?* I was ready for a great discussion! But Kurian rushed the students through the work of the day—reading articles on elected officials' plans to address gun violence and then filling out an accompanying sheet. This is not to blame Kurian but rather to acknowledge that structures of the school day (e.g., 50-minute class periods) limit possibilities for exploring imaginative responses to social problems. Nevertheless, within K–12 classrooms, educators like Kurian must intentionally resist those limitations so we can tap into students' abilities to dream up creative solutions to civic problems.

Even within these constraints, Kurian positioned his students as capable practitioners of civic discourse by designing a curriculum in which their expertise was valued and by creating a discursive space in the classroom where students could be themselves. Students did not have to make sure their contributions were correct or worded in a specific way before sharing; Kurian consistenly centered students' ways of knowing, speaking, and being within his curriculum and in classroom discussions. In fact, the kinds of language practices he encouraged that allowed students to participate could be done in any classroom as a civic practice, regardless of content area. His classroom was a place where many kinds of contributions were welcomed but still not a place where anything goes. Specific to his content objectives, he knew his students were capable of deep analysis, so he did not allow them to derail conversation with comments that he read as bad-faith distractions from their focus on social issues. In these ways, Kurian and his students were engaged in the practice of civics.

How might teachers in ELA classrooms draw from Kurian's example? How might we give students the opportunity to "leverage their everyday realities" in order to examine their existing worlds and imagine new ones (Mirra & Garcia, 2022, p. 350)? This work requires making space for students to share messy thoughts, allowing them to use "wrong" words to express ideas, and creating classroom communities where the norm is "we figure this stuff out together." After all, students are unlikely to truly share their own realities if they are not allowed to do so on their own terms. Looking at your own teaching to find opportunities to implement these ideas is how you can practice civic engagement and foster a classroom that works toward a democracy in the here and now.

Works Cited

Ahmed, S. K. (2018). *Being the change: Lessons and strategies to teach social comprehension.* Heinemann.

Clay, K. L., & Rubin, B. C. (2019). "I look deep into this stuff because it's a part of me": Toward a critically relevant civics education. *Theory & Research in Social Education, 48*(2), 161–181.

Garcia, A., & Mirra, N. (2021). Writing toward justice: Youth speculative civic literacies in online policy discourse. *Urban Education, 56*(4), 640–669.

Luke, A. (2004). Notes on the future of critical discourse studies. *Critical Discourse Studies, 1*(1), 149–157.

Mirra, N., & Garcia, A. (2020). "I hesitate but I do have hope": Youth speculative civic literacies for troubled times. *Harvard Educational Review, 90*(2), 295–321.

Mirra, N., & Garcia, A. (2022). Guns, schools, and democracy: Adolescents imagining social futures through speculative civic literacies. *American Educational Research Journal, 59*(2), 345–380.

Shalaby, C. (2017). *Troublemakers: Lessons in freedom from young children at school.* The New Press.

Taylor, L. A., & Hikida, M. (2023). Guest editorial: Introduction: Reconstructive discourse analysis as an approach to redressing racism in critical studies of literacy. *English Teaching: Practice & Critique, 22*(1), 1–10.

Zaccor, K. M. (2022). Connecting with students through a critical, participatory curriculum: An exploration into a high school history teacher's construction of teacher-student relationships. *Urban Education, 57*(5), 871–898.

Shifting the Paradigm of School-Based Writing: Teachers Using Journalistic Learning to Seed Civic Possibilities

CELESTE KIRSH

Introduction

Natalia was bothered. She sat in detention (again) for forgetting her uniform and noticed the same people in this middle school "time out." When our grade 8 class started to journalistically investigate issues in our local communities, Natalia knew what she wanted to research. Natalia (not her real name) started by interviewing classmates who were in detention often. She simply asked, "Does detention make you remember your uniform?" The answer was a resounding "No." She talked to the vice principal, who gave the usual adult rationale for the policy. After Natalia published her findings in our newspaper, something unexpected happened. The school quietly became lax about detentions. By the next year, the policy was nearly nonexistent. It was a small shift, but it revealed how powerful student journalism can be in sparking change.

This chapter traces aspects of the research that I conducted with teacher candidates, making the case that journalistic learning can allow teachers to reimagine the purpose and function of school-based writing for liberatory civic futures. To begin, I should clarify some concepts central to this chapter. Journalistic learning is when journalism is used pedagogically (Madison, 2015) and integrates civic education, media literacy, student agency, and more traditional writing pedagogies as well as newer forms of digital composing, positioning students as capable of meaning-making about issues that matter to them (Madison et al., 2023). Citizenship today increasingly involves activities such as volunteering, attending protests, engaging in online activism, or participating in boycotts. With a decline in more traditional, duty-bound ways of engaging civically, Clark and Monserrate (2011) argue that this signals a rise in more individually centered motivations for civic life. Through their research, they have found that participation in high school journalism affords students a sense of collectivism by practicing empathy, learning more about different groups within a shared community, and better understanding the costs and challenges of using your voice on behalf of the marginalized (Clarke & Monserrate, 2011, p. 418).

In what ways, then, can journalistic learning reimagine school-based writing for liberatory civic futures? This research expands the conversation of world-building civic education (Mirra & Garcia, 2023) and applies it to teacher learning, revealing that journalistic learning helps to foster the conditions necessary for civic inquiry, allows students to imagine themselves as capable of creating civic change, and provides an opportunity to "unflatten the other."

Conceptual Framing: A Lantern to Guide the Way

I put the data from this study into conversation with Mirra and Garcia's (2023) framework for world-building civic education. Mirra and Garcia (2023) explain that civic education is often framed as "participation in and engagement with existing structures" (p. 10) and yet it can also be thought of as interrogating what already exists and creating new possibilities. This framework for world-building civic education consists of five core classroom commitments—inquiry, storytelling, networking, imagination, and advocacy—which are encircled by youth agency, as well as by equity and justice (Mirra & Garcia, 2023. p. 11). These commitments get to the heart of what Mirra and Garcia (2023) see as the path toward new civic possibilities by asking deep and recursive questions such as: Why are things this way? Whose stories need to be heard? How can we connect with each other? What kind of future do we want to build together? How do we get there? (p. 14). These questions and classroom commitments are designed with student learning in mind, and yet my study focused on the learning of preservice teachers as a means of planting seeds for more hopeful classroom practices. The New London Group (1996) reminds us that "curriculum is a design for social futures" (p. 73), and if we believe this, then teachers are owed more experiences that center liberatory civic learning to eventually realize this future for their students.

Methodology

The site of this research was a 24-week, graduate-level course within the Master of Teaching program at the Ontario Institute for Studies in Education (OISE) at the University of Toronto during the 2022–2023 academic year. As part of their coursework, teacher candidates/participants took on the role of a journalist and interviewed one young person about their literacy practices inside and outside of school. With the data from this interview, teacher candidates created a short analytic memo that connected the literature in the course with the findings from their interview. Next, participants experimented through design sessions to expand their notions of what is considered a "text" and "writing." During these sessions, participants transformed their analytic memo into a digital journalistic text to share their findings. The range of texts included podcasts, TikToks/Reels, infographics, a virtual escape room, social media carousel posts, and memes. Following the composing of their text, participants wrote a reflection and were interviewed about their experience. While the digital composing aspect of this project was rich with insights and important findings, this chapter will focus on how teacher candidates constructed meaning through journalistic learning.

With the aim to personalize the data from this study, I center the themes of this research on three main voices: Ellen, Veronica, and Olivia (not their real names). What is shared by these three teacher candidates represents many voices captured in the data, and due to their unique characteristics and circumstances, their words are especially helpful at understanding the findings. All of the identity descriptors were written by the participants themselves.

Finding 1: Conditions for the Spark of Inquiry

Ellen, 23 years old, Korean, second-generation immigrant, Christian, heterosexual, female) almost exclusively read texts composed by white men while in school. When she realized the "canon of literature can include immigrant writers, can include East Asian writers ..." (Interview Transcript, October 23, 2023), it was only when she was an undergraduate. Ellen explains:

> . . . [including Asian/immigrant writers] can create a larger conversation about ways [students] can contribute to knowledge bodies and canons . . . it's about actually empowering student voice to be investigating, to be journaling, to seek out knowledge and have people take you seriously as an interviewer or as a researcher. (Interview Transcript, October 23, 2023)

When arguing for the importance of civic inquiry as one of the five core commitments of world-building civic education, Mirra and Garcia (2023) raise provocative questions: "Who gets to ask questions about society? Who gets to dream?" (p. 41). Ellen only saw examples of people asking questions and generating knowledge that reinforced existing power structures outside of her classrooms. For Ellen, the hidden curriculum of school-based writing was to explore *other people's* contributions to knowledge bodies, and East Asian people like her were excluded from asking the kinds of questions that produced knowledge.

While Mirra and Garcia (2023) aptly point out that "questions are the spark of social action" (p. 37), if students never see examples of people like them asking these questions, the spark for igniting social change may never be lit. What precedes a spark—the conditions required for a flash of fire to crackle into being—are equally important to consider. When educators commit to employing journalistic learning in their classrooms, they are inviting their students to inquire about their local communities and are validating that student questions are worth pursuing. When journalistic writing is published, it tells students that their voices deserve to be heard. Moreover, seeing examples of other student journalistic writing reinforces the idea that people like them are capable of contributing to funds of knowledge. Even if these "bodies of knowledge" exist solely inside a middle school—like Natalia, who opened this chapter—producing writing that has the express purpose of sharing knowledge with others tilts the purpose of school-based writing to "question society and tackle whatever shortcomings they find with a spirit of equity, empathy, and justice" (Mirra & Garcia, 2023, p. 37). The conditions necessary for inquiry that Ellen shares, facilitated by seeing diverse contributors to knowledge, illustrates the empowering effects of validating diverse narratives. This theme of empowerment continues next with Veronica, whose journey into journalism reshaped her identity.

Finding 2: Re-Storying Ourselves for Inquiry

Veronica (white, Christian, heterosexual, female) was in a unique position to be starting her second career as a teacher. Before teacher's college, Veronica worked in news media and wrote for TV. Similar to Ellen, she quickly made the connection to her own experience with school when reflecting on journalistic learning and noted how embodying an inquiry stance as a journalist required her to take an active role in her learning. Veronica explains:

> . . . When I turned about 11, I got weird and shy and hidden and passive in that way you do when you're a girl . . . And so any kind of journalism that you give to students, it forces them to be active. They have to come up with questions, and they have to actually talk to another human being . . . I think it is the opposite of passivity; you have to be very active in order to do any kind of journalistic learning. (Interview Transcript, June 28, 2023)

Veronica became the editor of her school paper, and she notes that having permission to go into the world to ask questions of people was transformative and contrasted with the ways that society taught her to be a woman. She reflects:

> I can ask questions of maybe even people in authority . . . there is no such thing as received wisdom. . . . [It is] all directly against how we're trained to be women. Be quiet. Don't ask questions. Don't speak. Don't challenge authority. . . . It was awesome, because I was, like, *Here's a pen and paper, Veronica, go around and ask people questions,* and I was so shy, but it was good. It got me out of my shell. I think it's brilliant. (Interview Transcript, June 28, 2023)

Taking on the role of a journalist was a metaphorical permission slip to act as a confident, inquisitive, investigator of the world. It offered Veronica new possibilities for how to civically be in the world as a young girl. When she had the power to "ask [her] own questions . . . and then write up [her] version of the truth" (Interview Transcript, June 28, 2023), Veronica gained access to a power that previously was unavailable to her and set her life on a path toward writing, creation, and actively constructing a reality through words. As Mirra and Garcia (2023) reminds us with the world-building civic commitment of storytelling, ". . . we need to be able to imagine change—in ourselves, in others, and in society—before we can enact it" (p. 107).

Veronica's engagement with civic imagination was undoubtedly more subtle than the examples Mirra and Garcia (2023) share; however, by being tasked to write as a journalist, Veronica documents a shift that occurred *internally* when she needed to take her pen and paper and ask people questions. She needed to imagine herself anew in order to write as a journalist. Mirra and Garcia's (2023) words again anchor Veronica's experience. They write, ". . . we conceptualize the imagination as a deeply visionary and constructive capacity of the human mind, one that engages with rather than retreats from our existing society but refuses to concede to its inevitability or perpetual continuation" (p. 104). While they were not writing explicitly about this occurring on an individual level, the logic certainly applies to what was occurring for Veronica. By adopting an inquiry stance as a journalist, Veronica was engaging with the world around her and was refusing to concede not only to the way the world happened to be but also to her own continuation as a shy, hidden, and passive version of herself. Veronica was re-storying herself *for herself* in order to be able to engage with the active, participatory inquiry of journalistic learning. The experience of going out into the world as a journalist allowed Veronica to tell herself different stories about what it means to be a woman. "Sometimes we only come to see the power stories have over the conditions of our lives when those taken-for-granted tales are interrupted or remixed to reveal something new" (Mirra & Garcia, 2023, p. 58).

In Veronica's recollection, we see how the purpose and function of school-based writing can shift from merely documenting learning toward reimagining who we can be in society. As Veronica's words highlight, journalistic learning is more than a genre of writing; it can be understood as a *way of being*. When she adopted the stance of a journalist, Veronica was able to imagine herself anew–someone who is powerful and capable of asking questions of the world. This, for Veronica, was the first step toward creating the possibility of a new civic future.

Finding 3:
Rigorous Joy through Unflattening the Other

A resounding theme from this research was the revelatory experience teacher candidates had when interviewing a young person about their literacy practices inside and outside of school. Teacher candidates often held ideas of young people conceptually; however, when actually sitting across from a real human, more nuance emerged.

The journalistic learning task with this research project required participants to interview a young person in grades 7–12, and for Olivia (female, Persian, middle-class, non-practicing Muslim), this meant interviewing her younger sister. Adopting the role of a journalist, for Olivia, meant trying on new patterns of engagement and not interrupting her sister. And while this was a challenge for Olivia and meant actually stopping the interview at times to regroup, as she explains, "It was also so interesting, because [my sister] had [the same] English teacher [as me]. And so being able to see her point of view, and it being so different to the experience I had, was really interesting" (Interview Transcript, July 15, 2023). She explains that "not being able to say anything, and just listening to [my sister] and asking questions, and not really giving my opinion, was probably the hardest bit. And I think that's because the nature of our relationship is that she says something and I say three things back to her" (Interview Transcript, July 15, 2023). Interestingly, Olivia's experience of sitting in the discomfort of another's truth had an unlikely result. Olivia says it best when she reflects: "But it's actually really fun, like, the whole interview process of being able to hear her point of view and stuff" (Interview Transcript, July 15, 2023). In addition to the situation being uncomfortable, irritating, and frustrating, what surfaced for Olivia was joy. It was *fun* for her ideas to be challenged. She ultimately enjoyed the process of hearing her sister's story and understanding a person she, very likely, had taken for granted and was used to dismissing.

When we think of civic education and classroom-based writing, typically analysis and argumentation come to mind, which are generally seen as hard academic skills, while empathetic listening and sharing stories are perceived as soft skills (Mirra & Garcia, 2023, p. 63). However, "joy" can be reframed as a "rigorous and serious pursuit" (Vlach et al., 2023, p. 121), meaning the empathetic listening that Olivia undertook as a journalist can take a different shape. Gholdy Muhammad (2023) explains that focusing on experiencing the truth of historically marginalized people and finding solutions to social problems can result in joy surfacing. Even if the patterns between Olivia and her sister meant that *Olivia* was typically the one marginalizing and silencing her sister (as anyone with a sibling might relate to), having the "vulnerable and humanizing" (Mirra & Garcia, 2023, p. 71) experience of careful listening was transformative for Olivia. That this experience was *fun* for Olivia should not be overlooked when we consider the power and value of journalistic learning and civic futures. "Joy is a special enlightenment of the heart and mind" (Vlach et al., 2023, p. 121), which is necessary if we are interested in transforming society through civic education. As can be seen by Olivia's experience, interviewing through journalistic learning unflattens the other, and by listening empathetically to other people's stories, the purpose of classroom writing can shift away from being predominantly focused on argument and analysis and instead toward the revelatory power of listening and, ultimately, joy.

Implications for the Classroom

Building off Ellen, Veronica, and Olivia's experiences, in this final section, I offer three possibilities for teachers to explore that leverage journalistic learning to reimagine classroom writing for more expansive civic futures.

Media Audit

To explore the idea that journalists have a civic responsibility to tell diverse stories, a media audit can be a powerful practice. You could use physical copies of a local newspaper, a media outlet's account on social media, or a news site, and in small groups, students document who they see and who they do not see. Categories can be constructed with your students or could be related to existing topics of study. With my students, we considered: gender, visible race, ages of people, body types, visible socioeconomic classes, physical abilities, visible LQBTQIA+ people, and visible religions. Following the media audit, students can write reflectively about any of these follow-up questions: *Why do you think some groups are overrepresented in this media? Do you notice any patterns about the people represented? Whose stories/images are missing? Do you feel represented by this media?* This experience is designed to serve as a provocation for student journalists to seek out stories that were not told in the media that they analyzed, moving closer to the ideal that diverse stories can be added to our canons of knowledge and that student writing has the power to rewrite limiting stories in order to foster the conditions necessary for civic inquiry to take place.

Writing and Thinking

When Veronica stepped into the role of being a journalist, she had to try on a different way of being and thinking in the world. Classroom teachers, regardless of their subject matter, can draw specific attention to the cognitive tools that different kinds of writing require. The thinking that is required for creating a collection of poetry is distinct from the thinking needed to produce a lab report. Students could take a draft of writing—for example, a report about affordable housing—and engage in roleplaying scenarios as different writers. How might a podcast host write with the research? How would a TikToker share this information? How might a documentarian express their thinking? How could a comedian write about this topic? More than writing in this role, transposing a piece of writing across multiple genres and modalities invites students to think expansively about civic issues through writing, and the different cognitive lens they try on through this experience can help to unlock different approaches to understanding and transforming civic problems.

Empathetic Interviewing

Journalists are trained to empathetically interview people who think differently than they do, sharing the stories of others in a clear, accurate, and unbiased way. Whether or not students are actually producing journalistic writing, the act of empathetic interviewing is transformative and applies to many disciplines. Students could interview an adult working in a STEM field, a local business owner, members of the soccer team, or an elder in their family, all with a variety of curricular objectives. A transformative thinking and writing prompt from Harvard Project Zero (2019) to use after the interview is: "I used to think . . . . Now, I think." This framing helps students to understand the shifts that take place when we listen with curiosity and empathy to others. Instead of analysis and argumentation being the primary ways students write to engage with civic education, how might our collective civic futures be less polarized if we instead centered *listening* as a political alternative (Gallagher & Kushnir, 2022)?

Looking back at Natalia's story opening this chapter, as a journalist she did not see how her writing created a more just system in her middle school, since the changes her writing inspired went into effect after she graduated. We can do better. When we intentionally set out to use classroom writing as a tool to create more liberatory civic futures, young people come to know that their words have power and can spark meaningful change. This should not be a surprise, like what occurred with Natalia's journalistic writing, but a core component of all our classroom writing in order to intentionally build the world we hope to come.

Works Cited

Clark, L., & Monserrate, R. (2011). High school journalism and the making of young citizens. *Journalism, 12*(4), 417–432. https://doi.org/10.1177/1464884910388225

Gallagher, K., & Kushnir, A. (2022). *Hope in a collapsing world: Youth, theatre, and listening as a political alternative.* University of Toronto Press.

Garcia, A. (2018). *Improving digital practices for literacy, learning, and justice.* International Literacy Association.

Madison, E. (2015). *Newsworthy—Cultivating critical thinkers, readers, and writers in language arts classrooms.* Teachers College Press.

Madison, E., Wantz, M., & Guldin, R. (2023). *Language arts in action: Engaging secondary students with journalistic strategies.* W. W. Norton & Company.

Mirra, N., & Garcia, A. (2023). *Civics for the world to come: Committing to democracy in every classroom.* W. W. Norton & Company.

Muhammad, G. (2023). *Unearthing Joy: A guide to culturally and historically responsive teaching and learning.* Scholastic.

New London Group. (1996). A pedagogy of multiliteracies: Designing social futures. *Harvard Educational Review, 66*(1), 60–92.

Ritchhart, R., Church, M., & Morrison, K. (2011). *Making thinking visible.* Jossey-Bass.

Vlach, S. K., Lentz, T. S., & Muhammad, G. E. (2023). Activating joy through culturally and historically responsive read-alouds. *The Reading Teacher, 77*(1), 121–130. https://doi.org/10.1002/trtr.2203

Grappling with the Glossary: Inspiring Civic Literacy Inquiry through Vocabulary Definitions

GRETCHEN HOHMEYER

Introduction

As teachers, we know that big inquiries can start with small questions. While completing a different research project (Hohmeyer, 2024), I read a George Washington informational picturebook (Herwick, 2012) twice because I thought something was off. The reason? The book referred to African Americans at Mount Vernon as *workers*. This might seem a slight difference, but the implication is stark. In informational texts, children often encounter words or concepts of disciplinary literacy for the first time (Ladd, 2012). Children reading this text would conflate enslavement with *worker*, a term usually associated with having wages and a certain amount of rights—when nothing could be further from the truth.

The terms *slave* and *plantation* have recently taken rhetorical turns. *Slave* is often replaced with *enslaved*, a reparative semantic turn to reclaim the agency and personhood of the enslaved. This is now common practice for agencies such as the National Park Service (2022). Rodriguez and Swalwell (2021) note that *plantation* is a "problematic euphemism" for "slave labor camps" (n.p.). The implementation of the Common Core, particularly its heavy emphasis on nonfiction texts, changed how children's books are structured (Isaacs, 2012). I became curious about how these terms were being represented to our youngest readers through the glossary of these texts.

Interrogating the definitions of words and layouts of books may seem like English language arts (ELA) instruction, but as Mirra and Garcia (2023) remind us, "all teaching is political and all teachers are civics teachers" (n.p.). Labeling an enslaved African American a *worker* is a political act that obliterates the realities of their lived experience and obfuscates the lessons of that history for today's children. Yet it is not surprising that the glossary is often overlooked. The simple list of bolded words with short definitions likely seems one of the least complicated back matter elements, often placed after the colorful maps, timelines, and extra information that comes after the main text. However, the ways young children learn vocabulary influences how they see the world. The words we use are infused with definitions decided by the cultural context in which we learned them. It is a cultural practice fraught with ideological implications. Mirra and Garcia's (2023) model of world-building civic education supports educators in creating more just futures, but we must consider the tools with which we build. We say much about the world we are attempting to construct for our youngest readers through the glossaries in their informational texts.

This chapter uses the glossary as a basis for civic and social justice inquiry through the ramifications of the definitions (or lack thereof) of the terms *plantation* and *enslave(d)* in sixteen children's (ages 4 to 12) informational text biographies on George Washington (see Table 1). Understanding how we define *plantation* and *enslave(d)* becomes even more contentious as numerous legislative efforts seek to dismantle teachers' ability to teach about racialized history. In a sense, these bills can give individual states or locales the ability to define these words differently. Children's informational texts can represent this difference in both image and text and may affect how children understand their world's historical and cultural implications for years.

Defining an Informational Text

While informational text is within the nonfiction genre, the terms are not interchangeable. Children's nonfiction may include illustrations or narrative, while informational texts focus on realistic, historical images and expository writing. Unlike narrative picturebook biographies, informational texts have complex page layouts that usually include various elements and text styles. However, the inquiry opportunities presented here are not only for informational text—they can be used anywhere there is a glossary.

Table 1. Book list of children's informational texts on George Washington

1. Aloian, M. (2013). *George Washington: Hero of the American Revolution.* Crabtree Publishing Company.
2. Bailer, D. (2017). *George Washington.* The Child's World.
3. Bolden, J. (2021). *George Washington: First president of the United States.* Children's Press.
4. Britton, T. L. (2017). *George Washington.* Big Buddy Books.
5. Britton, T. L. (2021). *George Washington.* Checkerboard Library.
6. Gaines, A. G. (2021). *George Washington: Our 1st president.* The Child's World.
7. Gregory, J. (2015). *George Washington: The 1st president.* Bearport Publishing.
8. Hansen, G. (2015). George Washington. ABDO Kids.
9. Herweck, D. (2012). *George Washington.* Time for Kids.
10. Kawa, K. (2018). *20 fun facts about George Washington.* Gareth Stevens Publishing.
11. Levy, J. (2019). *Before George Washington was president.* Gareth Stevens Publishing.
12. Mara, W. (2013). *George Washington.* Children's Press.
13. Murray, L. K. (2020). *George Washington.* Pebble.
14. Nelson, M. (2012). *The life of George Washington.* Gareth Stevens Publishing.
15. Olesen, A. (2016). *George Washington: America's history maker.* PowerKids Press.
16. Ransom, C. (2019). *George Washington.* Cody Koala.

Glossaries are only one of the elements used to help scaffold young children's understanding of complex texts, but they are often created uniquely for children. Ladd (2012) found that the glossary was one of the top three most common features in children's nonfiction, while it was the least common feature in adult nonfiction (p. 11). There is an understanding that these complex words must be explained more thoroughly to children. Rather than simply defining a word, a glossary can be a child's first introduction to important concepts or topics. Therefore, what is defined—and how it is defined—is critical to understand. However, teachers currently have almost no information on the connection between general vocabulary development and the glossaries in nonfiction texts. This chapter offers one way to understand what the glossary is doing and how it works so that educators can critically engage with their students on the topic.

Choosing Washington—and How to Choose Someone Else

Informational texts on George Washington generate critical examples of the power of a glossary, given his prevalent portrayal as a national hero. Biographies on Washington often serve more than one purpose: they discuss his life while framing him as a symbol "incarnating national values and character" (Hutchins, 2011, p. 649). Washington's preeminent status as the "Father of Our Nation" means that these books sometimes focus so much on creating a specific image of the United States that they forgo accurate details of Washington's life, such as exaggerating the truth of Washington's will (Hohmeyer, 2024). Telling the truth about Washington's lesser qualities can be seen as an attack not just on his legacy but on what it means to be "American."

This legacy must be disrupted to build a better civic future. As Fields and Fields (2022) note, the deliberate erasure of historically marginalized groups can only continue if we "create and re-create it in our social life, continue to verify it, and thus continue to need a social vocabulary that will allow us to make sense . . . of what we ourselves choose to do now" (pp. 147–148). If Washington's legacy is so pervasive, it is up to us to imagine a new way to tell the story that does not obfuscate the truth of the American history of enslavement. The destructive imaginary act of telling the founding of America as if it could be told without the enslaved "sucks away oxygen from the constructive imagining that we urgently need" for speculative world building (p. 289).

Washington is certainly not the only person whose biography is often co-opted for other motives. Rodriguez and Swalwell (2021) note similar issues in portraying the so-called Founding Fathers, leaders of the Civil Rights Movement, and suffragettes. Consider how this work might be done in the classroom with any glossary using critical literacy, which is about reading "both the word and the world in relation to power, identity, difference and access to knowledge, skills, tools and resources" (Janks, 2013, p. 227). Critical literacy tenets help us build better futures because they require taking action against oppressive systems (Mirra & Garcia, 2023). Unfortunately, biographies have a long history of sanitizing people's lives into flat representations that intentionally silence marginalized history (Kozol, 1975). Certain studies have found that informational texts have a particular sway with children, as, "unless they are told otherwise, children expect that what they read and hear will be true" (Isaacs, 2012, n.p.). Civic inquiry in this realm asks students to be critical of both what is being defined and how it is being defined across a corpus of many glossaries. In this example, these books create similar structures of Washington's life, yet the way they are constructed, the words that hold them together, and the world they produce can be very different.

A Tale of Two Terms: *Plantation* and *Enslave(d)*

I located in my library system sixteen Washington texts that defined 240 glossary terms. Within those 240 entries, forty terms were repeated two or more times. *Plantation* was defined four times over the sixteen titles, and *enslave(d)* was defined twice.

The Fraught History of *Plantation* and Mount Vernon

All sixteen books included information about Washington's plantation, Mount Vernon, but only four used *plantation* as a glossary term (see below). These four did not have many similarities. They are from various publication years, from 2012 to 2021, and are all from different publishers. Herweck (2012) fell on the low end of the reading levels while Aloian (2013) was the highest-leveled book. Thus, while some of the sixteen books had similar reading levels or came from the same publisher, none of those similarities are represented here.

The similarities come, instead, in the definitions. As expected, they are longer and more nuanced as the reading level increases. However, despite this, they use some very similar words. Across all four, the defining characteristic of a plantation is that it is *large*. The second defining characteristic is that a plantation is a large *farm*, a word used in all but Aloian (2013), which uses *agriculture*. One notable exception is Herweck's (2012) definition, which calls the labor force *workers*. As noted at the beginning of this chapter, suggesting that enslaved people could be

Table 2. Books that define *plantation* in the glossary (emphasis added)

Title	Lexile Level	Definition
Aloian, M. (2013). *George Washington: Hero of the American Revolution.* Crabtree Publishing Company.	1050	a large estate supported by agriculture; in the colonies often supported by slave labor
Britton, T. L. (2017). *George Washington.* Big Buddy Books.	600	A large farm
Gaines, A. G. (2021). *George Washington: Our 1st president.* The Child's World.	870	A plantation is a large farm or group of farms. Mount Vernon was the name of George Washington's plantation.
Herweck, D. (2012). *George Washington.* Time for Kids.	560	very large farms with many crops and workers

conflated with workers or employees is a negligent merging of terms. This is far from the reality of being owned by another human being and considered property, not people.

Herweck's (2012) text offers a brief example of how many books undercut their use of the term *farm*. Using their background knowledge, children will likely assume the prototypical rural set up with rolling fields and a red barn. This image is often in direct conflict with the images of Mount Vernon used in the text, which shows the large, white manor as the main building, with no farmland to be seen. In the two-page discussion of plantation life, Herweck (2012) writes that "George was a good farmer. . . . To improve his plantation, he set up fisheries, a mill, and an ironworks" (p. 16). The historical painting shows George, well dressed, standing off to the side while African Americans work in a field. The facing page has an extratextual box that describes what those three "Plantation Businesses" are, along with images of a mill building and a historical drawing of African American women at work on a dock. Consequently, this image is titled "slaves working in a fishery" (p. 17). Despite only otherwise using *workers,* including in the glossary, *slave* is used here with no context. How are children to understand what a plantation is from the dissonance between the text, the glossary, and the images? A plantation clearly includes more than a large farm. George is not shown farming. The plantation laborers are called *workers* in all but one instance, in which *slave* is left uncontextualized in a single image caption. This is not an explanation; this is obfuscation. Critical civic literacy is needed to unpack this intentional confusion.

The defining feature of a plantation is its reliance on enslaved labor, yet only one glossary definition includes this information. However, Aloian's (2013) word *supported* has several different connotations. They may have meant that plantation life was carried, underpinned, or propped up by slave labor, but it could also mean that slave labor was help, aid, or assistance. While the first is more accurate, the second is friendlier—and the ability to sway one way or another is a point of obfuscation of the facts.

While some authors (Aloian and Gaines) offer expanded definitions of slavery in their texts beyond the glossary, the location of this information matters. Aloian (2013) offers the best representation of the truth of enslaved life at Mount Vernon within the text. On page ten, there is a paragraph in the main text titled "Slave Society." This incorporation contrasts with Gaines (2021), which has an extra-textual "Slavery" section (pp. 36–37). It highlights the institution but removes the information from the main text and leaves it in a liminal space after the end of the main text but before the start of the official back matter. Both texts engage in specific authorial strategies about where enslavement can be mentioned.

Enslaved: A Site of Silence and Reparative Semantics

None of the sixteen books used *slavery* as a glossary term. The books that do choose to define the institution use instead the word *enslave(d).* Using enslavement rather than slave has the express purpose of using active language and respecting the personhood of individuals to whom great harm was done. Given the cultural connections of this rhetorical turn, the two books that choose not only to use this term but also to bold it as a glossary term—when none of the other

Table 3. Books that define *enslave(d)* in their glossary

Title	Definition	First Use in Context
Bolden, J. (2021). *George Washington: First president of the United States*. Children's Press	held by another person and thought of as property, without the right to fair treatment	He [Washington's father] left George a small piece of land and 10 enslaved people (p. 7).
Murray, L. K. (2020). *George Washington*. Pebble.	to make someone lose their freedom	They [the Washingtons] had enslaved people to do the work on the farms (p. 6).

fourteen books do—do so as an intentional, culturally connected choice. However, the inclusion of the term does not always result in good use in context, as in the image below and the following analysis.

One of the immediate similarities between these two texts is how recent they are. The publication year most likely speaks to using the term *enslave* rather than *slavery* as something just filtering into the cultural consciousness of particular authors and publishers. Unlike the previous set, these books are of the same Lexile level: about 550, or mid-range. Table 3 includes their use in context partly to show how early in these stories (pages 6 or 7) these terms were first used. However, these books did not use *plantation* as a glossary term.

Their definitions do differ. Murray (2020) defines to *enslave* as "to make someone lose their freedom" (p. 30). *Freedom* is also a glossary term, defined as "being able to live the way you want" (p. 30). Placing these definitions together, to *enslave* results in "making someone lose the ability to live the way they want." Since the institution is not otherwise described much in the text, a reader trying to understand more from the glossary is left with the impression that enslavement may be more akin to not letting someone have dessert before dinner rather than inhumane ownership of a person's life. Bolden (2021) offers the best detail, defining *enslaved* as "held by another person and thought of as property, without the right of fair treatment" (p. 32). Again, however, this descriptive line is in the back matter and is not a part of the main text, taking away some of its power.

Despite using the word *enslaved*, Murray (2020) obfuscates more than some other books that do not. The first use, noted in Table 3, is accompanied by an image of Washington as a child, playing with white friends. The second and final use comes in the last paragraph describing life at Mount Vernon:

> George liked farming. Different crops were planted on his farm. They grew corn, wheat, potatoes, and turnips. A lot of this work was done by enslaved people. George also made the house at Mount Vernon bigger. (p. 15)

Buried in the center of the sentence is the truth that enslaved people did this work, but their labor is only referred to passively: "crops were planted," for example. In comparison, "George liked farming" and "George also made the house bigger." The accompanying picture drives these descriptions home, showing George alone at work. There are no images throughout the entire book of African Americans. This fact is odd, as images of Washington include African Americans more than any other founder (Bagneris, 2021). Someone intentionally found enough to fill an entire book and keep African Americans from its pages.

Despite having a better glossary definition, this passive language repeats throughout the Bolden (2021) text. Bolden uses *enslaved* only twice in the main text—once at the beginning (noted in Table 2) and once at the end when discussing how "Washington said that the 123 enslaved people that belonged to him should be set free after his wife, Martha, died" (p. 27). Only one African American visually appears, but not who and where one might expect. No enslaved labor is ever shown. Instead, an image of Phillis Wheatley is included on a spread about Washington as commander of the Army (pp. 14–15). While the extra-textual box on the left features another use of *enslaved*, it is also an incongruous inclusion. It is only tangentially related to the topic of the spread and seems only to show an enslaved African American who supported Washington and to whom he gave praise and thanks. This is not to say that children should not learn about Wheatley, but her placement here—and the reasons given for it in the text—require interrogation.

Conclusion

My findings show that glossaries do important, complicated, cultural work, and they call for critical work in the classroom. It also highlights areas of note. Passive language, for example, is a problem with a long history, likely to be found in any number of texts. In what other stories is truth elided in service of a larger ideological goal? Teaching students to recognize it in any form will boost their civic literacy for years to come. The interplay of images and text is also a power play, as shown in books that remove visual evidence of enslaved labor when they define *enslaved*. This type of inquiry helps students to question not only what (or who) is there but also what (or who) is not—and to question why.

These are only a few of the glossary terms from my study and only a few lines of inquiry. With other topics, glossaries, and speculative civic goals, the opportunities go far beyond this chapter. To begin your own journey, here are four possible inquiry strategies for your classroom:

1. Collect diverse texts with glossaries on the same person/subject. Ask children to compare the definitions of specific words.
    a. Ask: What are glossary terms? Why choose these words? How are their definitions (dis)similar? Do the definitions tell you what you need to know?
2. Compare the definition of the term with its representation in the text. This is especially fruitful if there are multiple images, like "plantation." However, the inquiry might be about where the word is used on the page (main text versus extratextual element).
    a. Ask: Where and how is this term used in the narrative? Does it match with the definition?
3. Ask your students to create their own

definitions. This can be done pre-inquiry and/or post-inquiry. (I like both because students' opinions will change and grow!)

   a. Ask: Do you like the definition in the book(s)? Why or why not? What do you think this word means? Why?

4. Ask your students what words are not included in the glossary and why they think that is. Students can create an alternative glossary with their chosen words and/or rewritten definitions.
   a. Ask: What important words are not included in the glossary? Why do you think that word was left out?

In their own conclusion, Mirra and Garcia (2023) quote these words of Ernest Morrell: "We fight with words, because words become action" (n.p.). The possibilities for civic engagement with the glossary is a fight *with* words and *for* words. Students can understand these words as a constructed choice using civic literacy skills. A plantation is not "a large farm," but most of the glossaries present it that way. The presence of *enslave(d)* in a glossary suggests progress that is undercut by a critical multimodal analysis, as the linguistic step forward seems to result in the disappearance of images of African Americans. We cannot, in the words of Fields and Fields (2022), continue to verify this deliberate erasure of African American history. When we interrogate and contextualize these words with students, we fight for words and the better futures our students might create with these deeper understandings of history.

Works Cited

Bagneris, M. L. (2021). Illuminating the shadows of "liberty": George Washington and Blackness in American art. *American Art, 35*(3), 2–14.

Fields, K., & Fields, B. (2022). *Racecraft: The soul of inequality in American life.* Verso.

Hohmeyer, G. (2024). History in the margins: Using critical multicultural analysis on nonfiction depictions of George Washington to create civic discourse. *Language Arts, 101*(6), 385–394.

Hutchins, R. (2011). Heroes and the renegotiation of national identity in American history textbooks: Representations of George Washington and Abraham Lincoln, 1982–2003. *Nations and Nationalism, 17*(3), 649–668.

Isaacs, K. T. (2012). *Picturing the world: Informational picture books for children.* American Library Association.

Janks, H. (2013). Critical literacy in teaching and research. *Education Inquiry, 4*(2), 225–242.

Kozol, J. (1975). Great men and women (tailored for school use). *Learning, 4*(4), 16–20.

Ladd, P. R. (2012). The availability of access features in children's non-fiction. *International Journal of Knowledge Content Development & Technology, 2*(1), 5–16.

Language of enslavement. (2022, July 2). National Park Service. www.nps.gov/frdo/learn/education/language-of-enslavement.htm

Mirra, N., & Garcia, A. (2023). *Civics for the world to come: Committing to democracy in every classroom.* W. W. Norton & Company.

Rodriguez, N. N., & Swalwell, K. (2021). *Social studies for a better world: An anti-oppressive approach for elementary educators.* W. W. Norton & Company.

"Xavier for President": Skepticism, Truth-Telling, and Self-Love as Civic Expression

SARAH RAPP

Youth participatory action research (YPAR) projects in school are still rare, but if you have seen them in action, then you probably remember the students' heightened sense of engagement, as well as the surprises that emerged along the way. McIntyre (2000) suggested three essential elements of YPAR: a desire to solve a community problem, an emphasis on individual and collective knowledge about the problem, and a commitment to help resolve the problem. In McIntyre's study, youth of color told "visual stories" with "community photography" as subjects rather than objects of research, a key principle of YPAR (Duncan-Andrade & Morrell, 2008).

YPAR draws from a Freirean (1970/2007) emphasis on praxis (reflection and action) in a "problem-posing" model of education. Not surprisingly, there are often tensions when it comes to fitting such student-centered, open-ended learning into the confines of school curriculum, which is more teacher-centered and linear. Additional tensions emerge from the inherently political nature of YPAR, which cannot be separated from the contexts and identities of everyone involved. These tensions warrant more attention so that educators can more deeply understand and more meaningfully implement social justice projects.

A growing body of research (Marciano et al., 2020; Ozer et al., 2013; Winn & Winn, 2016) acknowledges the complexity of power dynamics, ownership, and "buy-in" in YPAR. One specific aspect of youth social justice projects that is not talked about enough is that there are often voices of skepticism and negativity mixed in with the agency and hope that are more commonly reported. An exception is Hendrix-Soto's (2021) study of students who were contesting district leaders' decision to relocate their school, in which she writes that "the accumulated harm resulting from the persistence of racism in [their] lives made them skeptical about the power of critical action" (p. 17). Her response was to redirect the project's focus to include joy, creativity, and a more attentive audience (brainstorming and envisioning the new school with the architects), but at least one student remained understandably resistant. I have also found that in such projects, there is frequently at least one student who stands out because they question whether or not the project can actually make a difference in the world.

In the YPAR project described in this chapter, one such skeptic, Xavier[1], a self-described "latinx teen from Cali," shaped the course of the class project, deepened its meaning, and shifted his teacher's and my (as a researcher) perspectives on the importance of skepticism. Xavier and others' contributions also illuminated the ways in which the teacher and I needed to be more self-aware and also transparent with students about the impact of our own whiteness as we endeavored to lead youth of color in a project focused on fighting racism. All educators and researchers, and especially those of us who identify as white, can learn from the ways in which Xavier's participation reframes skepticism as truth-telling and, in doing so, forges a path toward more authentic civic engagement for youth inside and outside school.

The Project

It was the second wave of the COVID-19 pandemic, the country was in upheaval due to the right-wing attack on the US Capitol and increasing reports of anti-Asian racism and anti-Black police violence, and Sophia Dinelli's grade nine English class was on Zoom for the second semester of the 2020–2021 school year. In an effort to increase student engagement online, Sophia had agreed to collaborate with me for my dissertation study about students' literacy learning in YPAR. We designed an open-ended process in which students could identify issues that mattered to them, do research, and take community action. As longtime friends and colleagues, we were aligned as we enthusiastically shared our plans with the students.

Many of the students met our excitement and positivity with their own, and the first few class discussions were lively as students discussed different project topics and implementation ideas. They chose their topic of racism through a class vote and began discussing what they could do. Their ideas focused on anti-Black and anti-Asian racism, which was noticeable because the majority of the students were themselves Latinx.

1. All names are pseudonyms chosen by the participants.

Xavier's Perspective: Opting Out of Optimism

Xavier was unique. He was not always in class, but when he was there, his voice was powerful. He unmuted himself often, usually to share an alternative opinion to what was being discussed. He offered critiques of ideas and plans that were suggested by the other students, Sophia, and me. He exuded confidence in his own knowledge, and in those moments, it seemed as if everyone was paying closer attention and waiting to see what he would say next. Following one of these conversations, another student joked in the chat, "Xavier for president."

When Sophia asked students to get specific about their project ideas, Xavier spoke up first, commenting that he did not care for the class topic of racism. He said, "I don't know, I didn't really like this subject because I don't feel like you could do anything about it." Most of us seemed unsure of how to respond because he was challenging the premise of the projects. One classmate supported him by echoing his ideas in the chat, and another shared the view that the pervasiveness of racism was what had led to people not caring about the issue and feeling powerless. I responded by trying to shift the conversation back to what I thought was a more hopeful place, reminding the students that it was always possible to do something. I said, "Do we accept that it's a normal part of life—what do you think about that?" and ". . . Is there a small thing we could do that could help us to head in the right direction?"

Xavier then lamented that kids were racist because their parents were racist. This sparked some determination among his classmates to impact future generations. They talked about creating antiracist board games, music playlists, children's books, and merchandise, as well as conducting interviews with people of color that could be shared on YouTube. They intended to educate children about racism by critiquing existing media, texts, and products or creating new ones with better representation. Xavier brought up the issue of racism in Disney movies, saying, "In cartoons, even Disney . . . I know in the past they've had really racist things come up in their cartoons." The students' comments showed they were considering racism as both an individual and systemic problem. Despite his misgivings, Xavier signed up for two project ideas: writing a children's book and making merchandise.

Micaela's Perspective: Shifting to Self-Love

Xavier's attendance was spotty for the next month, and he was not in class on the day the students hosted a guest speaker named Micaela who worked on equity issues in the city and county. When a student asked Micaela for her ideas about fighting racism, she responded, "I feel like the best advice that I've gotten from people lately is about self-love, and it's about being super proud of where you're from and who you are—and making sure that people know that." Micaela talked about her identity as a Chicana and gave the example of teaching people how to correctly pronounce her name (which she had done for me when we were waiting together in a breakout room before class). It was clear that Micaela's visit impacted the students, who shared afterward that they appreciated her "kind heart" and "good information." One added in the chat, "[Now] that we learned more stuff, we can do the stuff we wanted to do, like the books."

Sophia and the students referred to Micaela's visit for weeks afterward. When Xavier returned to class, students were discussing the connections between systemic racism and their projects. Xavier said, "I find this pointless." When Sophia asked him if there was a project he would prefer to do instead, Xavier said, "I don't think my voice could have an impact on this world." Instead of trying to convince him that he could make a difference, as we had both tried to do previously, this time Sophia repeated Micaela's idea of self-love. Even though Xavier had been absent for Micaela's visit, the idea of being proud of his identity and culture resonated with him. He said,

> *Oh, I'm proud* of who I am, who my family is, where we come from, where we came from, where we are now. *I'm proud.* I'm really proud of my mom and my grandma, but I just don't think anybody would listen to me or someone with my color. But if they were more up there, more well known, a celebrity . . . but I just wanted to say I think this is pointless.

Sophia listened and then asked Xavier if he wanted to do a project that involved sharing his appreciation for his family. He said, "I'm good at speeches," and Sophia responded, "Once again, Xavier, you have given us another idea." She added "Self-Love/Family Appreciation Projects" to the Jamboard page. By the end of class, five other students had changed over to that project option.

Ultimately, ten students chose to work on self-love/family appreciation projects, which was about half the students who usually attended class. These projects unfolded in individual ways, but all involved family interviews or presentations to relatives. The students who interviewed their parents, especially about immigration experiences, reported that the experience was powerful and made them more appreciative of their parents. The students also wrote final essays about what they had learned, and one student said he wanted to send his essay to Micaela.

It was unclear whether Xavier ever gave a speech to his mother and grandmother. However, his participation, and more specifically the doubt he expressed, represented an important turning point for the class projects. Xavier's skepticism fostered students' critical thinking, our own learning about deeper listening and the value of incorporating other voices, and alternative project options that were more relevant because they involved students' identities and contexts.

We Were All Learning

Xavier taught us more than we taught him. Because the class project took place in a high school English class, it began as a pedagogical approach focused on "academic literacy" and student empowerment. However, the joint work of the students, guest speaker, teacher, and researcher prompted the expansion and evolution of the projects that was needed for students' voices to truly be heard and for them to take personally meaningful action. Skepticism, truth-telling, and self-love were central to this work.

Skepticism as Truth-Telling

Initially, and without fully realizing it, Sophia and I were encouraging students to be hopeful and discouraging them from being skeptical. Though our intention was to help them feel better, we were inadvertently oversimplifying complex issues and dismissing students' knowledge and lived experiences of racism. It made sense that Xavier would view racism as insurmountable, since our country has never existed without it. Perhaps Xavier needed to say that contesting racism was very difficult because we did not say it enough.

Xavier's comments also drew attention to the fact that he, and most of the other students, had a different relationship to racism than Sophia and I did. With the students, we talked about racism abstractly, but we did not talk enough about our own whiteness. Though we discussed this amongst ourselves, with the students we might have even downplayed our differences, as in my comments that aligned myself with students in asking what "we" could do about racism.

Because Xavier continually resisted our invitation to get involved in the ways we were expecting, Sophia tried an alternative approach. At first she simply listened, which validated his experience. She also gave him choices and, recognizing the limits of her own perspective, brought in Micaela's advice instead. This resonated differently with Xavier. His passionate response assured us that he already felt pride in his family and culture and did not need us or the class assignment to foster this pride. He maintained that most people of color's voices are not heard in our society, and we can extend his critique to schools as part of society. By telling this truth, Xavier simultaneously and paradoxically created space for more voices.

Self-Love as Action

In order for the projects to be meaningful, Sophia and I knew the students' insider knowledge had to be honored, and they had to be in control of project topics, goals, processes, and products. Actually teaching in this way was much more challenging than we initially thought.

At first, most students did not share many personal experiences related to racism, which was surprising to us. Instead, they focused on the racism that other marginalized groups experienced. We were not sure if they were reluctant to share with us as white adults, with peers they had only met on Zoom, or if they did not see racism as relevant to their everyday lives because they lived in a segregated part of the city with people who mostly looked like them.

The class topic of racism was chosen by a vote, so it was not a preferred topic for everyone. Xavier and several other students expressed their dislike of the topic. We did not offer these students different options because it would have been more difficult for us to support multiple topics. Some of the students who had not initially voted for the topic of racism said that they became interested once the projects got going. Xavier and a few others continued to express that it was not their first choice.

The explicit goal of the projects was to fight against racism in society. Our assumptions of what constituted a school project and what constituted social action came together in our initial expectation that students would make something to present to strangers. Some of the students were enthusiastic about making a playlist or board game, but there was also a lull in the overall class momentum until Xavier returned to class.

Xavier assumed the role of expert and was recognized as a leader by both his peers and the teacher. The class was not the same when he was absent, and his comments made all of us think more deeply about barriers and possibilities. When he shared his pride in his family, Sophia offered an option to take that into the project. These personal projects were different from what we had initially envisioned. They made sense because the topic itself was so personal, and during the pandemic, the students' homes and families were the center of their worlds.

The other students may not have been as vocal as Xavier in their skepticism, but it is telling that so many of them switched to family projects after Xavier's conversation with Sophia. Micaela's suggestion that these students could take action by loving themselves was well received by the group because it took into account their identities and contexts. Their family struggles, resiliency, and strengths were honored. In the racist contexts in which they lived, self-love was a radical and critical act. In this project, positioning students as experts required flexibility and a departure from impersonal academic goals and linear timelines. As a result, the projects that emerged were unpredictable and more meaningful.

Implications for Civic Futures

Boyte's (2018) public work pedagogy emphasizes rather than avoids the complexities and tensions in youth civic education. Disagreement and challenges prepare students for working to make change in a diverse democracy. From this viewpoint, skepticism and debate are the foundations of a healthy democracy, and Xavier was engaged in civic work by pointing out the persistent obstacles that maintain systemic racism. In Freirean (1970/2000) terms, Xavier was not a problem but rather a "problem poser." He engaged in reflection and action as a "curious and critically thinking civic [agent] on [his] own terms" (Mirra et al., 2015, p. 15) within and beyond school.

As a "pedagogy of voice" (Safir & Dugan, 2021), YPAR can be understood as a pedagogy, a research methodology, and an alternative epistemology that values youth knowledge (Caraballo et al., 2017). We initially viewed the project in this study as a pedagogy, but youth epistemologies became more important than our preconceived ideas of teaching and learning processes and products. Caraballo and colleagues emphasized this view of YPAR in order to encourage YPAR's continual evolution. They also distinguished among four entry points for YPAR: academic learning and literacies, cultural and critical research, youth development and leadership, and youth civic engagement. This was another area in which the project evolved: academic literacy learning required that students also engage with their cultural, critical, and civic literacies. This required a new focus for both the students (self-love) and us (self-awareness).

Micaela brought us all back to the most important part: valuing the youth themselves. Filipiak (2023) wrote that the procedures of YPAR are much less important than the preservation of youth dignity, which includes creating opportunities for love and joy. This sort of dignity fuels civic action and needs to extend to young people's families and communities, especially those who have been harmed by traditional school pedagogy, policies, and practices.

In order for YPAR to fulfill its potential as a culturally sustaining, antiracist pedagogy, educators must engage in an ongoing process that Sealey-Ruiz (2022) calls "the archaeology of the self," which "involves the self-exploration, probing, and understanding of where issues of race and racism live within" (p. 24). As white adults facilitating a project about racism, Sophia and I took tentative steps in this direction. The ideas in the next section emerged from our reflections about how we (and others) could lean into this essential work more courageously in the future.

Classroom Applications

In the previous sections, I have interpreted what happened in the class project to make connections between civic expression, skepticism, truth-telling, and self-love. In what follows, I offer some suggestions for teachers doing this important, difficult, and joyful work.

Be Surprised

Give yourself and your students the opportunity to explore an issue and see what happens. You can have supportive structures ready (such as starter questions, graphic organizers, and project work logs), but do not begin a project with the end in mind. Students need to determine what matters to them and what should be done. The more student-centered the project, the messier and more unpredictable it is likely to be (from an adult perspective, anyway). The messiness contains multiple, varied, and unexpected opportunities for learning. Trust that your own knowledge and your students' knowledge will guide you.

Be Honest

Students have good reason to be skeptical of youth social action projects. Obvious inequities in our schools and society persist, and students understand that progress is complex and difficult. As adults, we vacillate between doubt and hope ourselves, so we should not diminish or gloss over students' mixed feelings or critiques. If we convince or require students to maintain a hopeful perspective, we are not being honest, we are not listening, and we are attempting to control students. In these moments, we can invite students into dialogue instead. Rather than being a stopping point, skepticism can open doors to deeper thinking and project alternatives.

Be You

Our identities and contexts shape how we relate to project topics. It would have been interesting to see what would have happened if we had more explicitly discussed our privilege and whiteness as adults in this study. In the teaching I have done since this project, I have focused more on acknowledging my own positionality and limited vantage points. Students seem to appreciate the ways in which this reconfigures them as the experts.

Being honest about our identities also helps identify curricular gaps and address them. Sophia was strategic in bringing in a guest speaker whose identity was a closer match to that of most of the students. We cannot assume that one person's experience represents anyone else's, but in this case, having a different perspective created an important shift. Students who had not previously discussed racism in relation to their own identities were willing to get more personal and vulnerable when the projects were framed as self-love rather than community action.

Be Together

The previous three recommendations are difficult, and educators would benefit from collaborating with other educators engaged in youth social justice projects. Because of the open-ended nature of this pedagogy, we cannot predict all of the challenges and opportunities that will arise. Teachers can reflect and share ideas about navigating these tensions and offer each other support, alternatives, and suggestions. Making space for this sort of professional dialogue goes beyond practical help and creates a community of critical friends who can work together to prioritize youth voices and transform schools into more equitable places.

Making Room for Skepticism (and Hope) in Youth Social Justice Projects

Xavier saw "buying in" as "selling out," and we learned so much from his contributions to classroom conversations and to broader societal conversations about racism. Xavier's skepticism taught us to shift 1) from mandated hope to truth-telling, 2) from oversimplification to complexity, 3) from experts to learners, and 4) from narrow and depersonalized academic goals and linear timelines to personal, flexible, iterative, and emergent work. All educators, but especially white educators engaging students of color in critical work, should look for the skeptics and listen more deeply to them. Rather than being a barrier in youth social justice projects, skepticism can be leveraged into meaningful civic expression, a hopeful outcome after all.

Works Cited

Boyte, H. C. (2018). *Awakening democracy through public work: Pedagogies of empowerment.* Vanderbilt University Press.

Caraballo, L., Lozenski, B. D., Lyiscott, J. J., & Morrell, E. (2017). YPAR and critical epistemologies: Rethinking education research. *Review of Research in Education, 41*(1), 311–336.

Duncan-Andrade, J., & Morrell, E. (2008). *The art of critical pedagogy: Possibilities for moving from theory to practice in urban schools.* Peter Lang.

Filipiak, D. (2023). Dreaming toward dignity: Nourishing self-worth, value, and well-being through youth participatory action research (YPAR). *Voices from the Middle, 31*(1), 23–27.

Freire, P. (2000). *Pedagogy of the oppressed* (M. B. Ramos, Trans.). Continuum. (Original work published 1970)

Hendrix-Soto, A. (2021). Activating joy and hope in critical literacies instruction: Responding pedagogically to youth skepticism in a YPAR project. *Literacy Research: Theory, Method, and Practice, 70*(1), 349–368.

Marciano, J. E., Peralta, L. M., Lee, J. S., Rosemurgy, H., Holloway, L., & Bass, J. (2020). Centering community: Enacting culturally responsive-sustaining YPAR during COVID-19. *Journal for Multicultural Education, 14*(2), 163–175.

McIntyre, A. (2000). *Inner-city kids: Adolescents confront life and violence in an urban community.* New York University Press.

Mirra, N., Filipiak, D., & Garcia, A. (2015). Revolutionizing inquiry in urban English classrooms: Pursuing voice and justice through youth participatory action research. *The English Journal, 105*(2), 49–57.

Ozer, E. J., Newlan, S., Douglas, L., & Hubbard, E. (2013). "Bounded" empowerment: Analyzing tensions in the practice of youth-led participatory research in urban public schools. *American Journal of Community Psychology, 52*(1–2), 13–26.

Safir, S., & Dugan, J. (2021). *Street data: A next-generation model for equity, pedagogy, and school transformation.* Corwin.

Sealey-Ruiz, Y. (2022). An Archaeology of Self for our times: Another talk to teachers. *English Journal, 111*(5), 21–26.

Winn, L. T., & Winn, M. T. (2016). "We want this to be owned by you:" The promise and perils of youth participatory action research. In S. Green, K. Burke, & M. McKenna (Eds.), *Youth voices, public spaces, and civic engagement* (pp. 123–142). Routledge.

INDEX

ABOUT THE EDITORS

Antero Garcia is an associate professor in the Graduate School of Education at Stanford University. His research explores the possibilities of speculative imagination and healing in educational research.

Nicole Mirra is an associate professor in the Graduate School of Education at Rutgers University. Her research utilizes participatory design methods in classroom, community, and digital spaces to collaboratively create civic learning environments with youth and educators that disrupt discourses and structures of racial injustice and that creatively compose liberatory social futures.

Stephanie M. Robillard is an assistant professor in the Justice, Community, and Leadership Department at Saint Mary's College of California. Her research explores Black girlhood, youth participatory action research, and antiracist teacher education.

ABOUT THE AUTHORS

Daryl Axelrod received his PhD in education from the University of Miami in Coral Gables, Florida, and is currently a learning specialist at Columbia University's Disability Services, a part of Columbia Health. His collaborative learning with digital literacies research covers two primary areas of interest. One is emergent bi-/multilingual students' multimodal composing practices, such as how adolescents use mobile devices to compose digital comics for literacy learning. He also examines youth and family storytelling practices that incorporate data visualization tools, such as families telling migration stories while examining related census data maps. His other line of inquiry concerns qualitative and quantitative research design accessibility, specifically for young adults with neurodevelopmental disabilities and autism.

Janelle Bence is a high school English teacher with twenty-four years of experience teaching in Texas. She is a longstanding member of the National Writing Project and enjoys collaborating with the Transdisciplinary Civic Learning Collaborative (University of Texas at Austin) and Colorado State Sustainable Teaching and Learning (Colorado State University). Her writing has been published in books including *Civics for the World to Come: Committing to Democracy in Every Classroom* (Mirra & Garcia, 2023) and *Teaching for Equity, Justice, and Antiracism with Digital Literacy Practices: Knowledge, Tools, and Strategies for the ELA Classroom* (Barnes & Marlatt, eds., 2024).

Glenda D. Chisholm is a postdoctoral research associate at Georgia State University, where she received her doctoral degree in Teaching and Learning. She uses critical ethnographic methods and participatory action research methods in her studies. In her current role, she works to understand the experiences of preservice and inservice teachers in a teacher residency primarily serving Black and Brown students. Specifically, in her work she seeks to understand the ways the residency has fostered a social justice educator orientation among residents.

Dr. Chisholm has over sixteen years of experience in education, working with students from primary grades to their postsecondary years in college, and she finds it incredibly motivating to work for a residency that seeks to prepare skilled, compassionate, and antiracist teachers. Because of her love for teaching and youth, she continues to work in her spare time in out-of-school spaces to cultivate youths' social and political awareness.

Minkyung Choi is an assistant professor in the Department of Teaching and Learning at Montclair State University. Her research interests include disciplinary literacy, narrative inquiry, and participatory action research. She can be contacted at choimi@montclair.edu.

Matthew R. Deroo is Associate Professor of Digital Literacies for Multilingual Students in the School of Education and Human Development at the University of Miami. In his research, Dr. Deroo seeks to learn with and from youth and their communities. His language and literacies-oriented research includes examination of the social and cultural contexts of immigrant and refugee youth; critical, digital media literacies; language education; and citizenship, civic engagement, and belonging.

Emma C. Gargroetzi is an assistant professor of STEM education in the Department of Curriculum and Instruction in the College of Education at the University of Texas at Austin. In her current research, Dr. Gargroetzi facilitates the Transdisciplinary Civic Learning Collaborative, a STEM-Humanities collaboration to explore the possibilities of classrooms as sites of civic imagination. She was a National Academy of Education and Spencer Foundation Postdoctoral Fellow (2022) and has published work in journals such as the *Journal of Teacher Education*, *American Education Research Journal*, and *Journal of Research in Mathematics Education*.

Gretchen Hohmeyer decided in 2016, while completing her MS in library science and MA in children's literature at Simmons University, to read one biography on every American president. Now having read over 200 books on American history and counting, she is a doctoral student in the Language, Literacy, and Culture concentration of the College of Education at the University of Massachusetts Amherst. Her research interests include elementary social studies education, children's literature, and otherwise unpacking the ways American history is imagined for children. You can find reviews of all 200+ history books (plus the fiction she reads for fun) on her YouTube channel, "Betwixt the Books."

Jennifer Kahn is an assistant professor of Teaching and Learning and Learning Scientist in the School of Education and Human Development at the University of Miami. Dr. Kahn studies how to broaden participation in interdisciplinary, technology-rich activities to support youth learning across school and community settings.

Jean Kim is a public middle school English teacher in Queens, New York. She can be contacted at jean@q300.org.

Celeste Kirsh taught middle school English and social studies for over a decade and is a PhD candidate at the University of Toronto/Ontario Institute for Studies in Education in the curriculum and pedagogy program. She is the host and producer of the podcast *Teaching Tomorrow.*

Diana Liu is a public high school English teacher in Brooklyn, New York, and an adjunct instructor. She is a PhD candidate in the English education program at Teachers College, Columbia University. She can be contacted at dyl2126@tc.columbia and on Twitter @MsLiu_in_Edu.

Lakisha Odlum is an assistant professor of English education at the City University of New York (CUNY) at Queens College, where she teaches undergraduate and graduate preservice and inservice teachers. Her research interests include the intersection of racial and digital literacies, culturally responsive teacher preparation, diversifying the teaching profession, and the teaching of Black girls.

Sarah Rapp is an assistant professor at Sonoma State University. Dr. Rapp teaches graduate and undergraduate students in the Educational Leadership program and in the Curriculum, Teaching, and Learning MA program. Before that, she was a high school English teacher and administrator in Santa Rosa, California. Dr. Rapp received her doctorate from the University of California, Santa Cruz. Her research focuses on the tensions and possibilities of Youth Participatory Action Research and other social justice pedagogies. Currently she studies what happens when educational leaders incorporate youth voices into their school improvement efforts.

Tyana Velazquez-Smith is an adjunct professor at the University of Rochester, where she teaches a course called Literacy and Social Practice. She is the CEO and founder of Sensational Inclusion, an education consulting company supporting neurodiverse, Black, and Brown students. Diagnosed as autistic in adulthood, Dr. Velazquez-Smith integrates personal experience and scholarly research to advocate for culturally sustaining and sensory-friendly teaching practices.

Her dissertation, titled *"Everything Can't Be White": A Love Story of How Black Girls Resist White Supremacy through Self-Love, Imagination, Play, Solidarity, and Joyful Literacy,* explores the resilience of elementary-aged Black girls in predominantly white schools. These students navigate and resist racist and sexist conditions that subject them to various forms of violence. While much research has focused on older Black girls, Dr. Velazquez-Smith's work highlights the often-overlooked experiences of younger Black girls and their use of literacy practices as resistance strategies during English language arts instruction. Her work aims to bring attention to these unreported and under-researched harms and the ways Black girls employ literacy to resist and make sense of their experiences.

Anthony Voulgarides has been an English teacher in New York City's grade 6 through 12 public school classrooms for the last twenty years. In addition to teaching, he is a doctoral student (EdD) and adjunct lecturer in English education at Hunter College, City University of New York (CUNY). Along with more traditional teaching of language and rhetoric, he uses project-based methods, youth participatory action research (YPAR), and media to make learning authentic. As a doctoral student at Hunter College, his research focuses on youth civic engagement, critical media literacy, and critical consciousness development. He can be reached at anthony.voulgarides02@hunter.cuny.edu.

Hyo Kyung Woo is an assistant professor of English at Texas A&M University-Commerce. Her teaching and research interests include multiethnic literature, transpacific postcolonial studies, and Afro-Asian studies. Dr. Woo is interested in incorporating global cultures and space-based learning in her classroom, where she regularly teaches the topics of linguistic justice, translingualism, K-pop, and various literary forms. Her article "Teaching K-Pop at an HBCU: The Possibility of Afro-Asian Solidarity" will be published in a forthcoming special issue in the *Journal of Multimodal Rhetorics (JMOR).*

Anisa Yudawanti is a doctoral student in Race, Inequality, and Language in Education at Stanford's Graduate School of Education. She is the proud daughter of Indonesian immigrants and was born and raised in Madison, Wisconsin. Drawing on her experience as a public school youth worker and high school social studies teacher, Yudawanti studies young people's racialized relationship to space and place at school. Her work explores youth of color's movement and navigational practices through the lens of everyday forms of resistance and refusal. Her broader research agenda engages with critical arts-based methods and socio-spatial re/counter-mapping of school space. She situates her current research in the Midwest and the Bay Area.

Karla Zaccor is an elementary school teacher in Chicago public schools. Prior to returning to classroom teaching, Dr. Zaccor was an assistant professor of language and literacy, at which time she did research focused broadly on educational equity and classroom talk about race in the context of the ELA classroom. She is happy to be back in Chicago (her hometown) working directly with young people. You can contact her at kzaccor@gmail.com.

This book was typeset in PT Sans, PT Sans Narrow, and Alternate Gothic No3 by Cynthia Gomez.

The typefaces used on the cover include Franklin Gothic Medium and Avenir Black.

The book was printed on 50 lb., white offset paper.